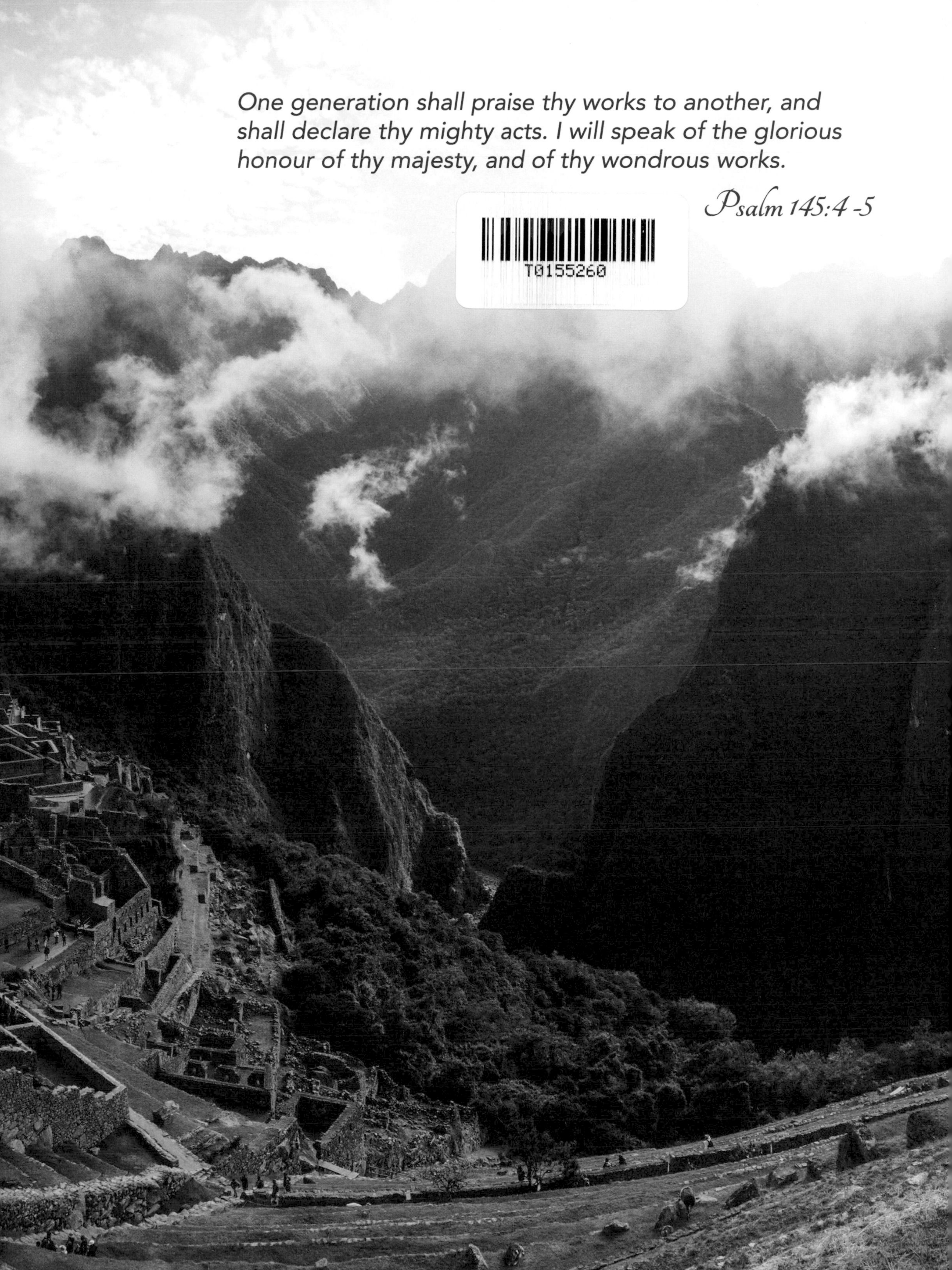

One generation shall praise thy works to another, and shall declare thy mighty acts. I will speak of the glorious honour of thy majesty, and of thy wondrous works.

Psalm 145:4-5

BRILLIANT

MADE IN THE IMAGE OF GOD

3275 Monroe Rd.
Midland, MI 48642
989-837-5546
www.searchforthetruth.net
truth@searchforthetruth.net

Brilliant.

Cover Design – Michael Malone
Interior Graphic Design – Jamie Walton, Michael Malone, Jill Gerhardt

ISBN: 978-1-939456-15-1
Library of Congress Number: 2014910701
First Edition - November 2014
Revised Second Edition - September 2015

Scripture references KJV unless otherwise noted

Printed in China

Search for the Truth Publication Policy:

The Bible has repelled every effort to discredit and distort its reliability for thousands of years. There are FAR more ancient Bible manuscripts than for any other historical document, and these manuscripts agree with modern verbatim translations to greater than a 99% accuracy. It is obvious the Bible is an incredibly historic and unique book.

A primary function of our publications is to demonstrate how well facts from both history and science fit a straightforward Biblical framework of reality. Factual errors occasionally creep into any book; however, there is never an excuse for distorting the truth to fit one's bias. Christianity and the Bible have nothing to fear from an honest evaluation of the truth. Please contact us if any of the information found within Search for the Truth Publications is found to be factually incorrect in any way. It is our policy to remove any factual errors from subsequent printings.

Photo Credits:

Cover – Public Domain, Michelangelo's Creation of Man from the Sistine Chapel
Bruce Malone - 14,56,58,60,62,64,76,80,86,90,92,102,110,112,116,118,126,back endsheet
Freeimages.com – 16,20,22,30,44,50,54,96,98,104,120,122
Gracewaymedia.com - cover/front endsheet, 10,26,42,78,106
Freerangestock – 6,36,38,82
Morguefile – 24,38,114
Lightstock.com - 2
David Lines (Creation Evidence Museum) - 24
Jamie Walton – 69,88
Google free use images – 32,48,70,84,124
Wikipedia free use images – 12,34,68,88,94,100
istockphotos.com – 18,40,74,108,124
Shutterstock.com – 46
Mark Armitage - 23
Jamshed Jurabaev (Deviantart.com) – 28
Dennis Swift – 52

Dedication

This book is dedicated to my grandchildren, Corrie, Eleanor, and Lillian, who will be growing up in this time of increasing deception and persecution. May they hold tightly to the truth as they make God's Word their firm foundation.

For over two thousand years Christians have been anticipating the return of Christ. At no point in history have the signs of the times set the stage for this event so eminently. A profound prophetic statement from 2 Peter 3:3-6 states that *"in the last days scoffers will come..."* The passage goes on to state that the primary attack on the truth of God's Word in these last days will be the denial of a literal creation of the universe and a literal world-covering flood upon the Earth. Today, these events are widely denied (including within many churches and Bible colleges). The exciting days in which we live are what the Bible refers to as *"The Last Days."*

Acknowledgements

Thanks to my wife Robin for all her help, encouragement, and patience. You are my best friend through life's adventures and my life would be incomplete without you. Thank you for all the love and support you have given me through the years. You are intensely loved.

This book has been brought to life due to the artistic talents of Jill Gerhardt, Jamie Walton, and Michael Malone. Thank you for the countless hours spent designing each page in a way to make it a visual masterpiece.

Without partnering with those far more detail-oriented than myself, *Brilliant* would be filled with errors. My special gratitude goes to my editors and proofreaders – Don and Jeri Slinger, Aaron Slinger, Claudia Malone, Bill and Carol McFarland, and Pam Koehlinger. The second edition was greatly improved by comments from Ralph Monroe, Sylvia Thompson, Patrick Corcoran, Bird Derrick, Roger Zakariasen, Sharon Brown Sivertsen, and Susan Davis.

Thanks to Lighthouse Church in Harbor Beach, MI, and many other individual supporters who funded 100% of the cost of the first printing of this book. This allows us to make copies available at a low cost for wide distribution to others. These supporters understand the importance of placing the truth of God's Word and the timeline of the Bible as a "shining light on a hill" for all to see. Without you, this project would not have been possible.

Brilliant Pages
Arranged within time period

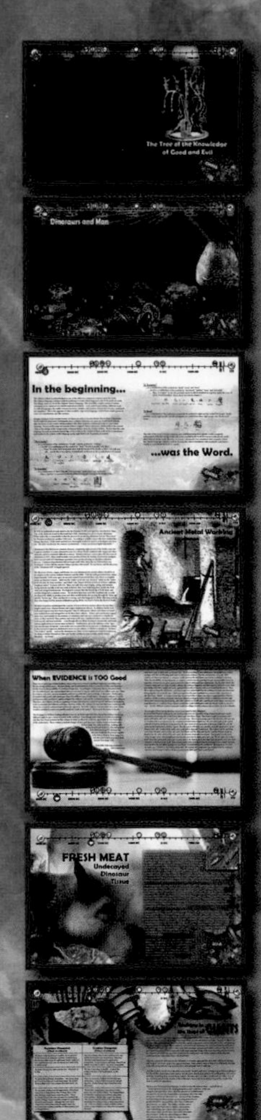

The Tree of Knowledge p.12

Dinosaurs and Man p.14

In the Beginning... Was the Word p.16

Ancient Metal Working p.18

When the Evidence is TOO Good p.20

Fresh Meat p.22

Walking in the Steps of GIANTS p.24

Not So Dumb Cavemen p.28

Cave Art p.30

The Original Mega Church p.32

Post Flood Cities p.34

Cutting History Down to Size p.36

The Real Population Explosion p.38

Ice Age Cities p.40

Firm Foundations p.108

The REAL Fake p.110

Surgeons of Peru p.112

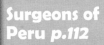

Shake, Rattle, and Roll p.114

Dinosaur Pots p.116

Machu Picchu p.118

Mankind in the Image of God p.120

End of Time p.122

Other pages

Introduction p.6

A Word about Time p.8

References p.124

About the Author p.126

Order Form p.128

4000 BC 3000 BC 2000 BC 1000

Pre-Flood World p.10

Dispersion of Humanity p.26

Rebuilding Civilization p.42

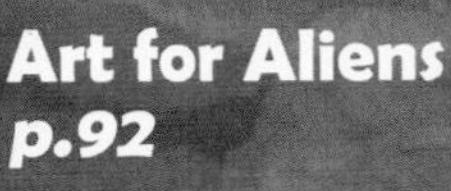

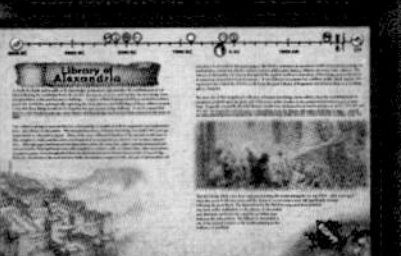

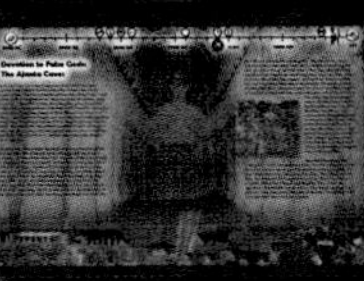
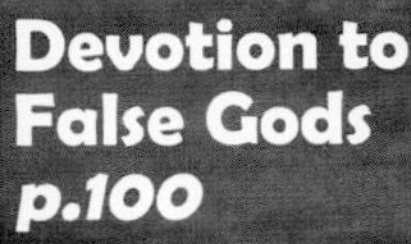
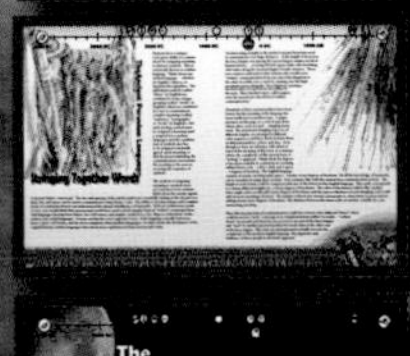

Mankind's Memory in Marble p.80
Greek Gods in Genesis p.82
Quiet Ancient Amphitheaters p.84
Holes in Your Head p.86
A Charge from Ancient History p.88
Underground Aqueducts p.90
Art for Aliens p.92
Army of the Dead p.94
But it's JUST Paper p.96
Library of Alexandria p.98
Devotion to False Gods p.100
Stringing Together Words p.102
Greek Computers p.104

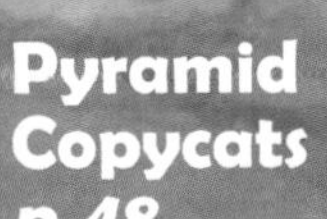

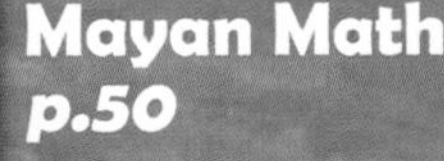
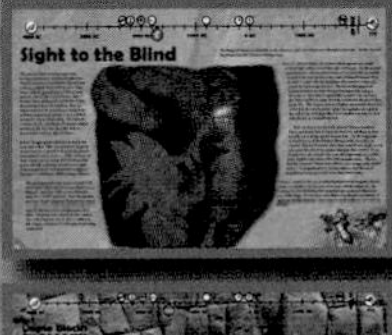

Mapping the Past p.44
Dying with Distinction p.46
Pyramid Copycats p.48
Mayan Math p.50
The Iron Age of Egypt p.52
Beautifying Technology p.54
Sight to the Blind p.56
Duplo Blocks for Giants p.58
Foundations of Civilization p.60
Massive Mining Operations p.62
The Original Coneheads p.64
Superhighway to the Past p.66
Landscaping *on a Massive Scale* p.68
Texas-Sized Marbles p.70
Movable Print p.72
The Real Native Americans p.74
Mound Builders p.76

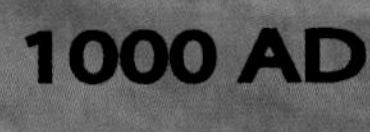

Technology Advancement p.78
Rise of Science p.106

The Key to BRILLIANT

History is important. What we believe about the past has a direct bearing on how we perceive the present and what actions we will likely take in the future. American founders Patrick Henry and Daniel Webster stated, respectively, *"I know of no way of judging the future but by the past"* and *"History is God's providence in human affairs."* This is why those out to destroy the influence of Christianity have worked for over one hundred years to remove references to the Christian faith from American history books. Christian faith principles were promoted by the vast majority of America's founding leaders. When generation after generation are misinformed about the importance that the Christian faith and the Bible played in the founding of America, they naturally assume that it must not be that relevant to our nation today.

The abilities and intelligence of early mankind are other areas where true history has been totally ignored, misinterpreted and/or rewritten. Throughout the academic world it is assumed to be a fact that mankind evolved from some less intelligent, ape-like forms of life. Yet if man did develop via some ape-to-man transformation, there should be an abundance of archeological evidence showing a gradual development of civilization – such as gradually increasing sophistication of building techniques, mathematics, language, artistic ability and scientific understanding. Evidence contradicting this viewpoint is hidden from students throughout our educational system.

The Bible clearly indicates that mankind was recently created in God's image and was highly intelligent from the very beginning. Jesus even stated, *"Have you not read that at the beginning He created them [people] male and female?"* (Matthew 19:4) Thus, from the moment of creation, people would have been capable of developing technology, complex languages/communication, and building projects. The purpose of this book is to document exactly these types of abilities throughout ancient civilizations.

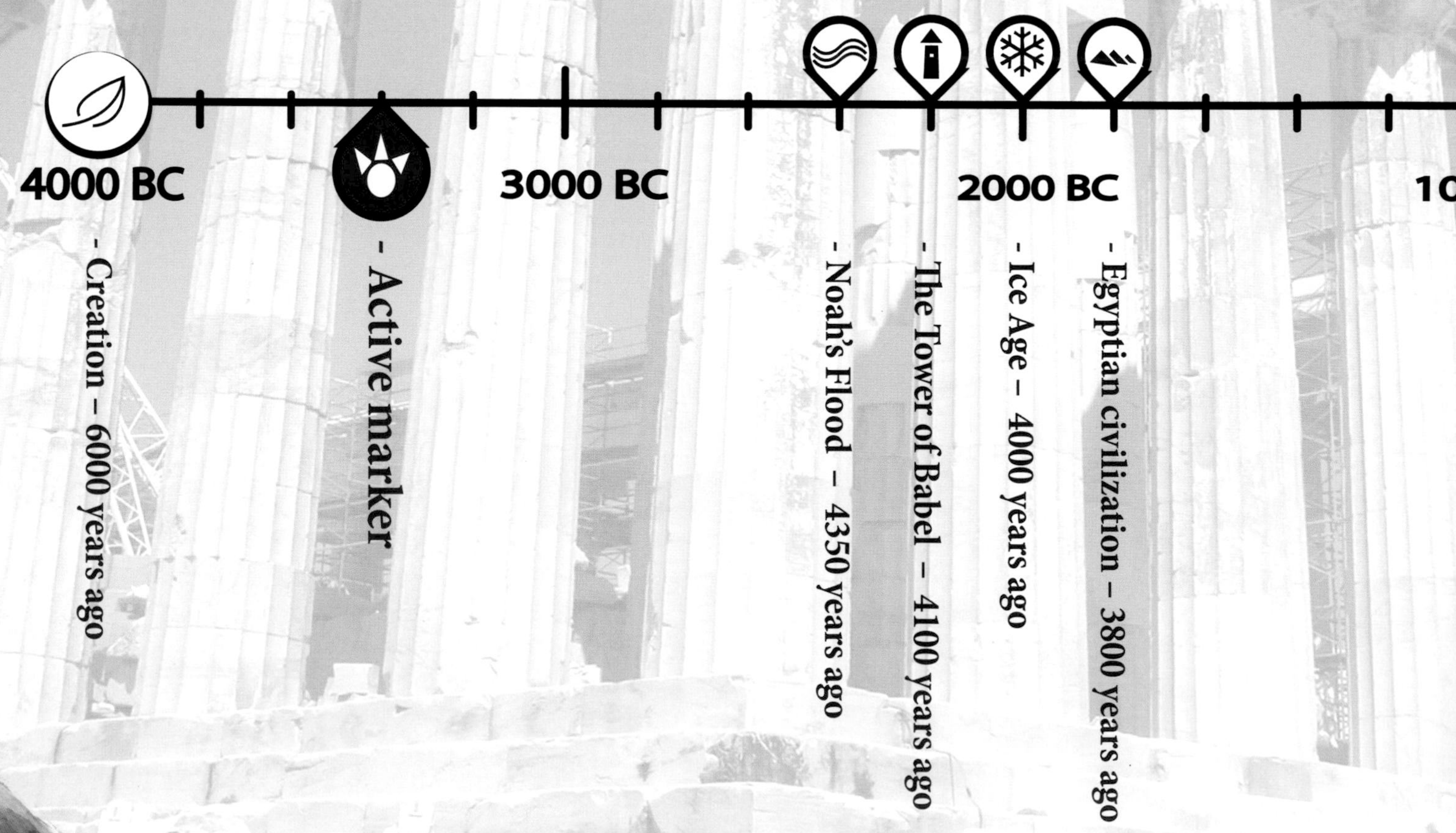

Understanding that people have been recently created in the image of God has enormous implications in every area of life. Even the founding of America is based on this historical reality. America's Declaration of Independence declares the very justification for our war to separate from England as the unalienable human rights of *"life, liberty, and the pursuit of happiness,"* - **endowed by a Creator**. Thus it is not government (i.e. a group of people in power over other humans), but the historical fact that humans were created in God's image, which establishes human rights. This is incredibly important. If our rights exist only due to governmental authority, then another group of people coming to power can just as easily remove these rights.

On each page of this book you will find both a timeline and a globe. ***THE COLORED AND HIGHLIGHTED SYMBOL*** within each will show at a glance where in time AND where on the planet the archeological feature documented on that page is found. In addition, the timeline pinpoints key civilizations and Biblical events so the context of each page can be understood in comparison to other historical events.

Note that the dates often used for artifacts or ancient cultures are only approximate, as there is much disagreement, even among experts, as to the correct dates for ancient cultures. In addition, carbon dating becomes increasingly inaccurate as we approach the date of the worldwide flood due to a shift in carbon levels throughout the Earth's biosphere during (and for many centuries following) the flood.[1] However, the best estimation of the age of artifacts which fit a Biblical time frame (i.e. adjusting for the misconceptions of evolutionary presuppositions) will be used throughout the book.

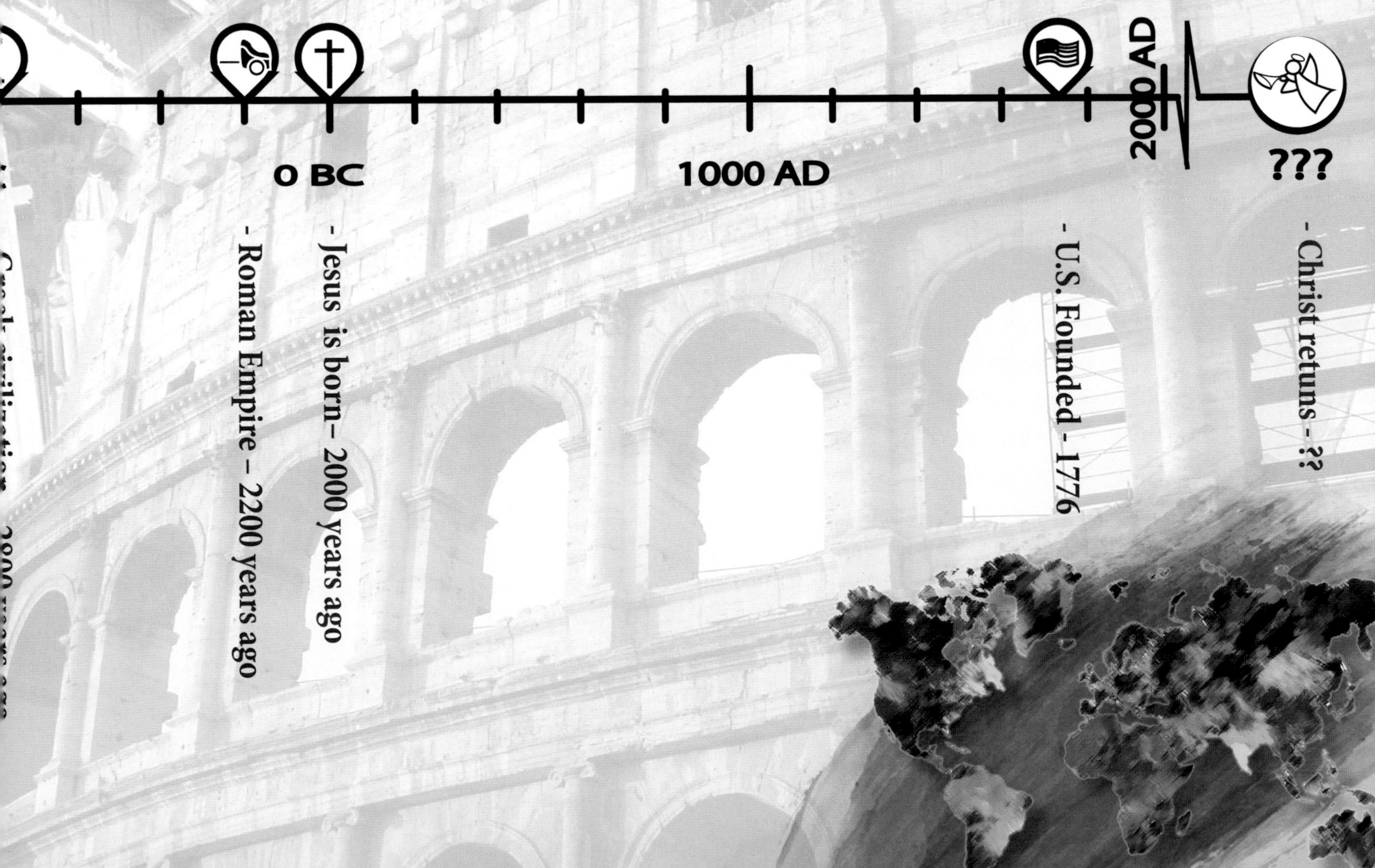

A Word About Time

I'm sure readers have already noticed that the timeline on each page of *Brilliant* starts approximately 6,000 years ago and terminates nearly 6,000 years later (close to our current time period). This is so startlingly unlike how people are trained to think about history that it is difficult to keep from automatically dismissing this timeline. But take a moment to ponder how our understanding of the past is determined.

A thousand years is an enormous gulf compared to a single human lifetime. How many of you know ANYTHING about your great-great-grandfathers? That was a person directly related to you only FOUR generations removed. (One generation is approximately twenty-five years.) Someone alive a thousand years ago is ten times as removed – FORTY generations previous. Only two hundred and fifty years ago America was a group of English colonies, traveling by horse and carriage was normal, sailboats ruled the oceans, no one could have conceived of electric lights or refrigeration, and people routinely "owned" other human beings as slaves.

As we go even further back in history our understanding of the past becomes clouded with guesses and colored with preconceptions learned from those who came before us. Probing possibilities outside of the "known" consensus thinking is always opposed by those who have committed their lives and careers to the "accepted viewpoint." Academic credibility is at risk, and few vary too far from the consensus. This bias becomes so strong that honest researchers become blind to any viewpoint other than the one they have come to consider as reality. The human mind is actually designed to interpret reality based on what it has been trained to believe to be true, to the point that our brains will unknowingly and automatically modify and misinterpret observations in order to fit them into firmly established paradigms. An enormous age of the Earth is a paradigm so strongly promoted (but only in the last 150 years of academic thought) that it has become almost impossible to consider any other possibility. Yet how exactly do we know the age of the various ancient cultures of the Earth?

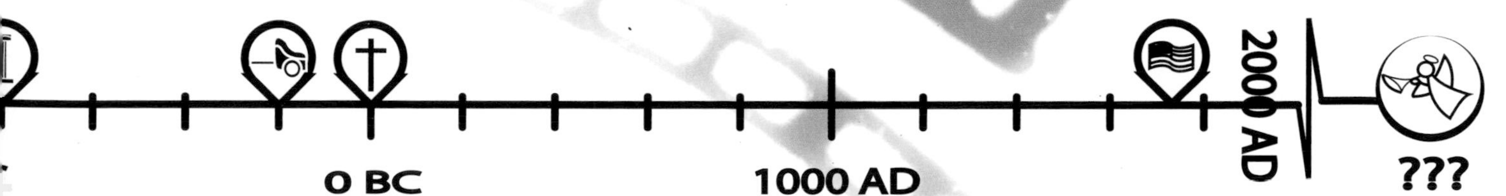

- Carbon dating is only as accurate as the assumptions upon which it is based and does not measure time but merely the amount of a certain type of carbon within an artifact. If there has indeed been a worldwide flood upon the Earth, it literally guarantees a shift in the carbon-14 level. This means that the "dates" of artifacts before and until a new equilibrium was reached (hundreds of years after this flood) are guaranteed to be wrong.

- The rise of most of the Earth's ancient cultures is strongly tied to when it is believed the Ice Age ended. If the Ice Age is misinterpreted, so is the dating of these cultures and artifacts. The Ice Age was an unstoppable consequence of the worldwide flood, so if this flood is denied, then the date of the Ice Age and the ages of these cultures will be misinterpreted.

- Documents from cultures themselves are also used to piece together the culture's age, but these records are often fragmented, speculative, and prone to exaggeration and creative interpretation. Conflicting evidence is forced into the paradigm of an ancient Earth like the cutting of jigsaw puzzle pieces to make them fit the preconceived cover of the box, and anomalies are covered up like smearing makeup over blemishes.

Even the author's attempt to set the age of artifacts and cultures discussed within this book is really quite speculative. Sincere and careful Bible scholars debate the date of Noah's flood - placing it anywhere from 4350 to 5200 years ago. In this volume we will use the most common and recent date for the flood - 4350 years ago. Although this may be too recent, the difference is trivial compared to the vast ages promoted by our educational system which is blinded by presumptions of evolution. It is quite likely that additional evidence will result in moving some of the indicated dates up or down this book's Biblical timeline. Yet no evidence has ever PROVEN the Bible's timeline inaccurate. And there is much evidence that casts doubt upon the extremely extended timelines required for evolution. This volume unashamedly takes the Bible as a credible source of history and attempts to show how known historical artifacts fit into its straightforward statements concerning Earth's history. In other words, *Brilliant* assumes the Bible means what it actually says, instead of assuming the Bible is completely wrong about the timeline of human history. I believe you will find fascinating how many archeological mysteries disappear when the evidence is examined from this logical and Biblical perspective.

THE PREFLOOD WORLD
6000 TO 4350 YEARS AGO

This period of Earth history covers the time from the creation of a perfect Earth environment through mankind filling the Earth with theft, violence, and murder. The end of this period brought a real, literal, world-reshaping water catastrophe upon the globe, which ripped up every land plant and killed all animals and humans not saved on the Ark of Noah. Many were buried to become fossils, coal, etc. EVERYTHING from the pre-flood world was *"deluged and destroyed"* (2 Peter 3:6). So what can we know of this period of Earth history? In this section there are a few reminders and human remembrances of this lost world: the origin of humanity and the origin of sin recounted within the original written symbols of the Chinese language; controversial human and dinosaur footprints testifying to the creation of man and dinosaurs together; a remembrance of the lessons from the Garden of Eden found within a 4000-year-old brass sculpture; and soft tissue still found within dinosaur fossils showing that the flood was, indeed, a real and recent event.

An amazing prediction of future events comes to us from almost 2000 years ago: *"Scoffers will come in the last days saying, 'All things have continued as they were since our fathers fell asleep...' " (2 Peter 3:4).* This prophecy goes on to state that these scoffers will deny two

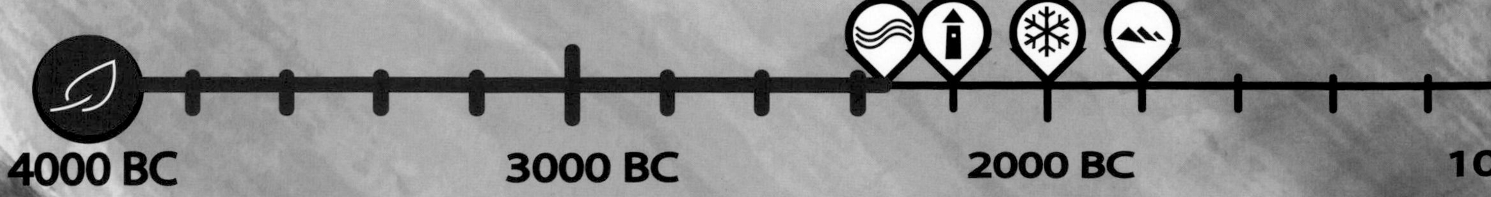

events which the Bible states are a fact of history - the reality of a literal creation of the Earth and universe and the reality of a real globe-restructuring flood (2 Peter 3:15). A primary reason that the Bible - and by implication, Christianity - has become noncredible to an increasing number of people is the systematic promotion of the idea that everything in the indefinite past has operated exactly as we see it operating today (i.e., *all things have continued as they were since our fathers fell asleep*). The Bible also states in clear, straight-forward language that during the period of Earth history from 6000 – 4500 years ago there were two incredibly significant interactions of God with creation.

The first interaction was when man, the only physical entity which was given total freedom to obey or disobey the Creator, decided to reject God's authority. Mankind had to be given this freedom or he would have been little more than a biological robot. Without freedom, there cannot truly be love. Yet the moment mankind chose rebellion over obedience, we were forever separated from a totally holy and totally just God. Thus, God devastated His entire perfect creation – bringing death into all of creation – so that we would not continue to live as biological creatures forever separated from Him. God then set into motion the plan of reconciliation whereby God, Himself, would take the penalty of death which we deserved (i.e. exactly as if the fair judge in a capital murder trial decided to take the death penalty deserved by the guilty person upon Himself after the sentence had been pronounced). Yet we know very little of this prefall creation -- where death did not exist.

The second interaction of God was during the worldwide flood. Approximately 1600 years after creation, this flood totally devastated and totally destroyed the preflood world. By examining the fossil record and the size of the coal seams of the current world (coal comes from plants, animals, and algae alive before the flood), we get a picture of the pre-flood world. The size and variety of these fossils and rock layers testify to a lush worldwide near-paradise that was destroyed. Furthermore, locked into the very rocks upon which we walk, visible to every culture around the world, is the timeless testimony that the ***consequence of sin is death***. Thus, this flood serves as an undeniable warning written in rock from a loving God to every subsequent generation.

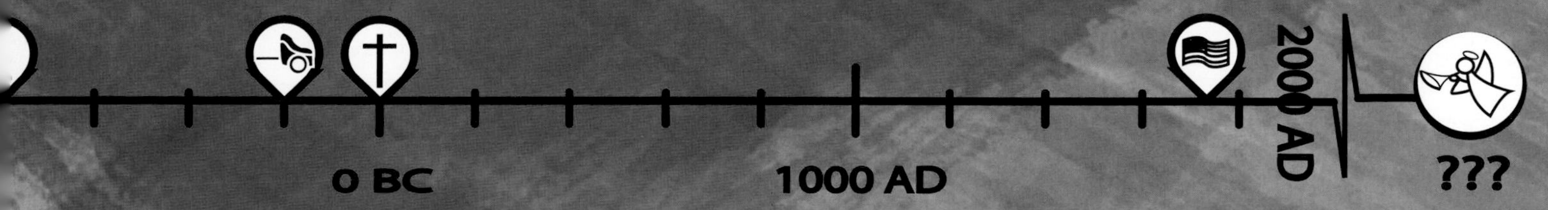

The Tree of the Knowledge of Good and Evil

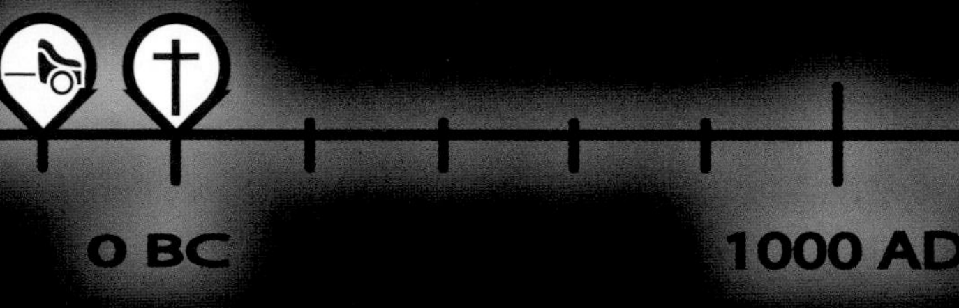

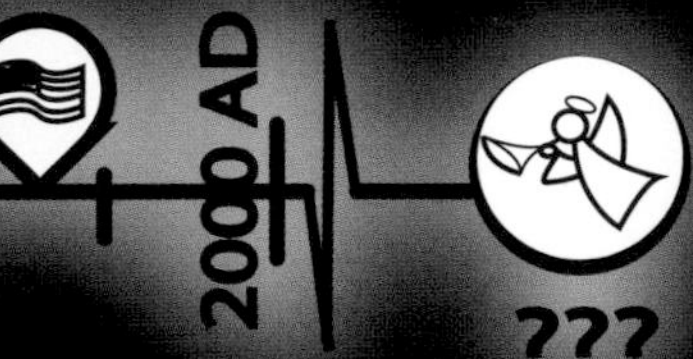

It is hard to even imagine what the original creation looked like before death began. God looked out over everything He had made and declared it not just good, but "*very good*" (Genesis 1:31). This was after the creation of mankind… but before mankind had brought sin into creation. If mankind were made billions of years after God started creating things, then Jesus' statement, "*Have you not read that IN THE BEGINNING He made them [humans] male and female*" (Matthew 19:4) makes no sense. Furthermore, if the geological layers of the Earth are the result of billions of years of slow accumulation (rather than resulting from a real world-restructuring flood 1,600 years after the beginning of creation), then God's definition of a "very good" creation is really hundreds of millions of years of death, disease, bloodshed, and extinctions.

The world-altering event which changed EVERYTHING in the original creation was mankind's disobedience of God by eating a forbidden fruit from a tree which God called the "*tree of the knowledge of good and evil*" (Genesis 2:17). Before this there was no evil in the physically created world (although Satan, a spiritual entity, had previously rebelled against God and been allowed dominion upon the Earth). The very laws of science by which the universe operated must have been different, and we can only speculate what the world and human abilities must have been like before sin distorted creation. Even after this act of rebellion, mankind's lifespan was over 900 years! It seems likely that before the fall (the entrance of death into creation), cell replication would have been absolutely perfect – with no mistakes as one cell divided into another. Thus, creatures would have literally and biologically lived forever. Perhaps regeneration speeds were also greatly increased, allowing almost instant healing of any damage. God alone knows.

What we do know is that humanity was given a choice to obey God or reject God's authority. When Adam ate the fruit from the forbidden tree he was essentially stating, "I don't want to obey God's rules. I want to make my own rules…. I don't want you to be God. I want to be God." At that moment God changed all of creation so that we would not continue to live forever but be forever separated from Him. It did not surprise God that we chose rebellion over obedience, and there could not truly be love if we had not been given a choice. So God set in action that incomprehensible plan whereby He would eventually become a perfect, sinless human and take the price of rebellion (death) upon Himself so that faith in His sacrifice would be the ONLY requirement to come back into fellowship with Him.

But is there any evidence that this momentous event – when mankind reached up into a tree to grab a forbidden fruit while being tempted by Satan in the form of a snake – is real? We find exactly that in an ancient bronze statue of a tree found buried in the ruins near Guanghan, China. This twelve-foot tall tree has sloping branches, but significantly, on the branches bearing fruit, the leaves are shaped like dangerous knives (indicating that the fruit of this tree is dangerous or forbidden). Coming from the very center of the tree is a long snakelike body, but this snake still has legs near its head and the snake is glaring down near a human hand with its large evil eyes and bared teeth. Lastly, the bronze statue has a human hand reaching toward the tree near the serpent's head.[1]

This huge bronze statue was cast at the very beginning of the Chinese culture – over 3000 years ago. It is obvious that, long before missionaries ever arrived in China, these original Chinese people (who were direct descendants of Noah) wanted their children to remember the factual event which brought death into all of creation. So they created a twelve-foot tall bronze tree memorializing one of the most significant events of all human history.

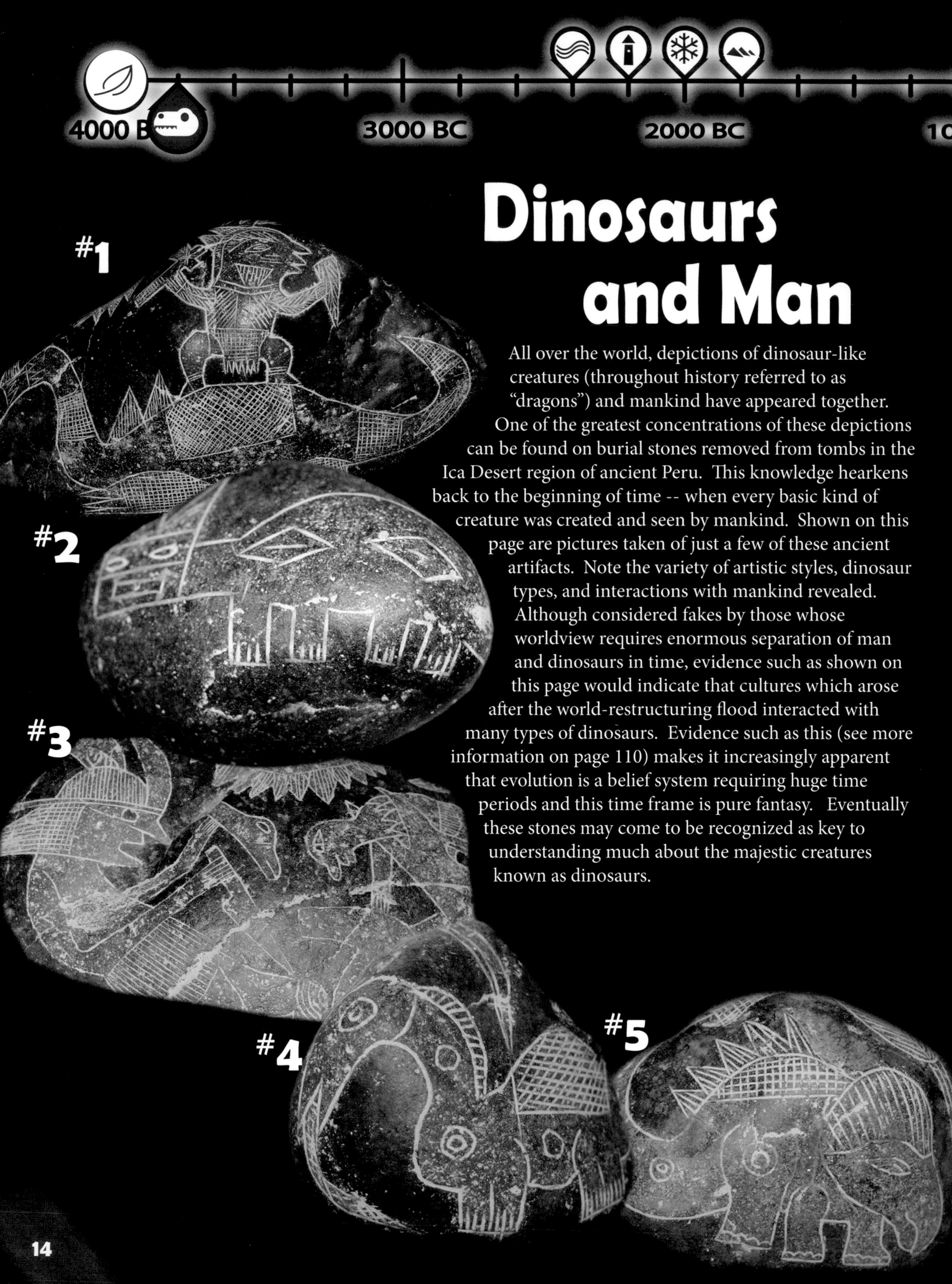

Dinosaurs and Man

All over the world, depictions of dinosaur-like creatures (throughout history referred to as "dragons") and mankind have appeared together.

One of the greatest concentrations of these depictions can be found on burial stones removed from tombs in the Ica Desert region of ancient Peru. This knowledge hearkens back to the beginning of time -- when every basic kind of creature was created and seen by mankind. Shown on this page are pictures taken of just a few of these ancient artifacts. Note the variety of artistic styles, dinosaur types, and interactions with mankind revealed. Although considered fakes by those whose worldview requires enormous separation of man and dinosaurs in time, evidence such as shown on this page would indicate that cultures which arose after the world-restructuring flood interacted with many types of dinosaurs. Evidence such as this (see more information on page 110) makes it increasingly apparent that evolution is a belief system requiring huge time periods and this time frame is pure fantasy. Eventually these stones may come to be recognized as key to understanding much about the majestic creatures known as dinosaurs.

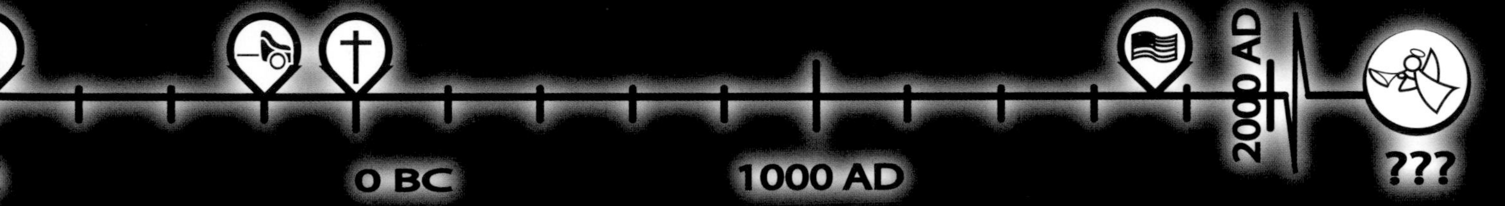

1. An ancient depiction of man's supremacy over even the greatest beasts of creation. Note how the tail is being held erect. Up until the 1980s, dinosaurs were depicted as dragging their long heavy tails on the ground. Dr. Jack Horner changed this perception of dinosaurs, and they are now shown walking about with tails held erect. This supposed "forgery" (and many other burial stones) shows the tail held erect; yet it was found at a time when all dinosaur books showed tails lying flat on the ground. Thus, this burial stone shows knowledge which no forger would have possessed.

2. Note the very different stylistic head on this depiction – obviously many different artists were involved in the carving of these ancient stones.

3. The battle scene depicted here involved multiple dinosaurs and people in mortal combat.

4. A fire-breathing dinosaur? Notice the circular skin markings. Skin impressions showing such circular patterns were not found until the 1990s; yet the stone carvings showing these circular skin impressions were collected as early as 1960.

5. Dozens of variations of stegosaur fossils have been found – this variation was carved before such a fossil was found and shown in literature.

6. Here is a yet-to-be-discovered type of dinosaur. Obviously this depiction was not taken from the picture in any modern book on dinosaurs. These stones have every indication of being authentic artifacts.

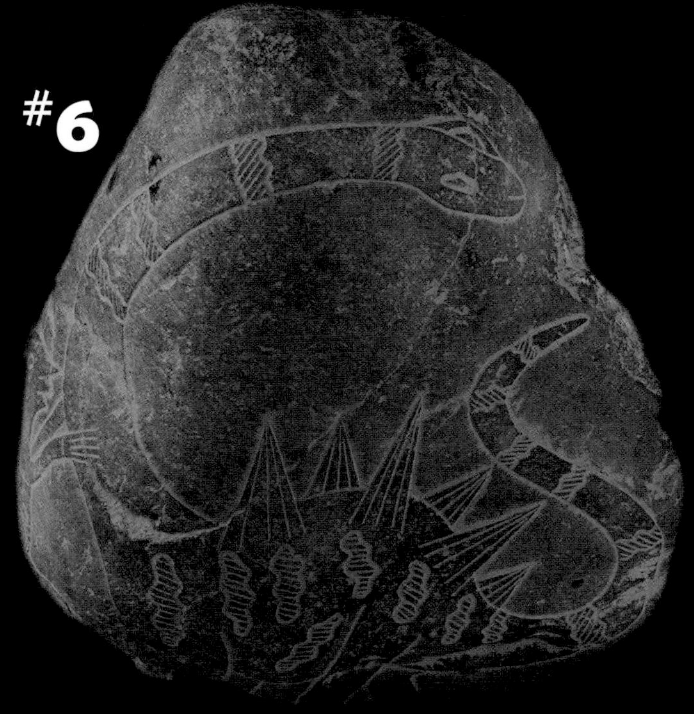

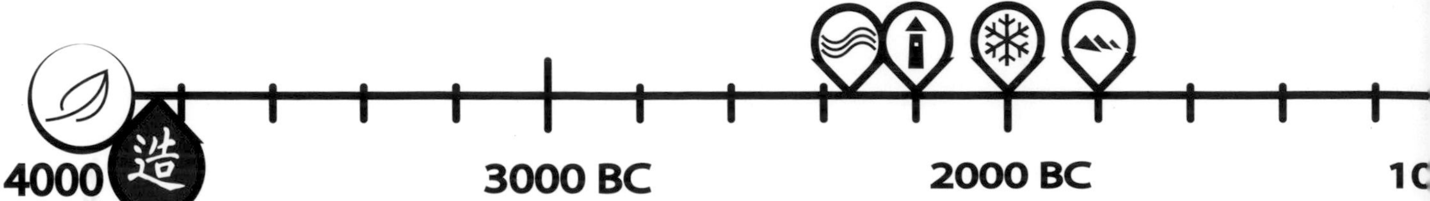

In the beginning...

The Chinese culture is acknowledged as one of the oldest in continuous existence upon the Earth. The Chinese language contains symbols testifying to events which happened early in the preflood world. This incredibly complex system of written communication contained over 80,000 individual symbols – each symbol representing a different word. As with all languages, the earlier version was more complex, and modern versions have become condensed and simplified. This is the opposite of what would be expected if languages evolved from simple grunts of some sort of prehuman, ape-like creature.

Imagine having to learn not just twenty-six letters in order to become literate, but needing to memorize 80,000 different characters! Fortunately, these complex characters are made up of individual symbols (like the letters of our words) which combine with other symbols or historical events to convey their meaning. Shown on this page are several of these original Chinese characters which testify to the ancient Chinese knowledge of the actual events of human history from the Garden of Eden. The fact that this early language has such an intimate knowledge of the events in the Garden of Eden could not be a coincidence and testifies to the origins of this language going right back to the beginning of creation. Apparently these Chinese were direct descendants of Noah who formed their written language based on events which happened early in Earth history.

"To Create"

…is a combination of the symbols for "to talk" and the symbol for "walking."

….“to talk" is a combination of the symbol for "dust," "breath of mouth," and "alive."

…Thus, "to create" is to bring dust alive with the breath of the mouth so that it can walk and talk – exactly like a description of mankind's creation from the second chapter of Genesis!

土	+	口	+	丿	=	告	+	辶	=	造
dust		*breath of mouth*		*alive*		*to talk*		*walking*		*to create*

"A Garden"

…is a combination of "dust," "breath," "two persons," and "enclosure."

…Thus, a "garden" is an enclosure where two people were given the breath of life.

土	+	口	+	亻亻	+	囗	=	園
dust		*breath*		*two persons*		*enclosure*		*garden*

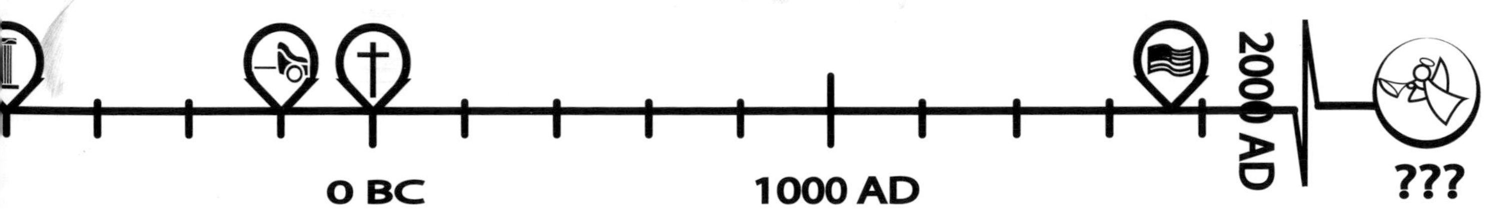

<u>"A Tempter"</u>

...is a combination of the symbols for "devil," "cover," and "trees."

... devil is a combination of the symbols for "movement," "garden," "man," and "privately."

... Thus, "a tempter" is one who privately moves to talk to mankind in a garden under the cover of trees. Sound familiar? If not, check out Genesis chapter 3.

ノ + 田 + 儿 + 厶 = 鬼 + 林 + 广 = 魔

(motion) garden man privately devil trees cover tempter

<u>**"A Boat"**</u>

...is a combination of the symbol for vessel with the symbol for eight and the symbol for people. Noah's ark held exactly eight people, and all of humanity descended from these eight people after the flood of Noah.

舟 + 八 + 口 = 船

vessel eight people boat

The odds of the exact concepts, numbers, and symbols forming these specific words, completely independent of the knowledge of the real events recorded in the book of Genesis, is ridiculously small. Ethel Nelson's classic work, *Discovery in Genesis* [1], documents over a hundred other examples of how the Chinese language contains symbols showing this culture's familiarity with mankind's early history – exactly as recorded in the book of Genesis.

...was the Word.

In 1952, an undisturbed tomb dated to the Jin Dynasty (1,700 years ago) was unearthed in China. One of the skeletons found in this tomb had a belt containing four pieces of pure aluminum. What makes this so remarkable is that the process for producing aluminum was not "discovered" by Western scientists for another 1500 years. According to reliable sources who have studied this unique discovery, "*[T]he tomb and belt were thoroughly studied by modern archeologists and chemists. The latter vouched for the existence of aluminum. A hoax was deemed highly improbable.*"[1]

Aluminum is the third most common element, comprising eight percent of the Earth's crust, but it appears nowhere as a pure element because it is always found combined with oxygen and other elements, and it is extremely difficult to extract. Modern reference sources place the discovery of aluminum at 1825, when small modules were produced from the heating of potassium amalgam, but it was not until 1854 that larger quantities were produced using an expensive reduction process. Commercial production did not begin until 1886, when the use of electrolysis was developed. So how did the ancient Chinese produce this metal? No one knows, and the discovery of the "aluminum belt" is largely ignored.

The discovery of iron, copper, and bronze (or even aluminum) by ancient cultures should be of no surprise to the serious student of history and the Bible. Only the sixth generation from Adam (approximately 5,600 years ago), an ancestor named Lamech had three sons whose accomplishments are listed in Genesis – Jabel was the "*father of all who raise livestock,*" Jubal was the "*father of all who play the harp and flute,*" and Tubal-Cain "*forged all kinds of tools out of bronze* **and iron** (emphasis mine)" (Genesis 4:20-22). Thus, not only were men forging, casting, and manufacturing intricate metallic tools very early in history, they were fashioning these metals into both wind and stringed instruments. It is logical to assume that this knowledge of both music and metalworking had a common source. Yet modern historians insist that mankind only recently developed the ability to produce iron and other useful metals after passing through the "stone age" and the "bronze age." How can they be so wrong, and what happened to all the older iron tools if they were being used by ancient civilizations going all the way back to before the flood of Noah?

Modern researchers misinterpret the scarcity of iron tools from ancient cultures because they largely rusted away, whereas bronze and copper implements did not. In addition, harder iron tools and weapons may have been of greater value to subsequent cultures and whenever found were melted down and reforged for use by these later cultures. Pottery and even bronze/copper items were used mainly for decorations or containers and were not considered as valuable for reuse, so they survived. Thus, pottery and stone tools were considered to have come first, bronze tools second, and iron tools last - even though all were likely developed concurrently and found various applications at various times in history. Furthermore, given the influence of the "ignorant ancient man viewpoint," even on the rare occasion that an ancient iron or aluminum artifact is discovered, it is ignored, attributed to more recent cultures, or labeled as misplaced. Yet these "out of place" metals are found in ancient ruins around the world - such as the aluminum in China or iron implements found from places as far-flung as Indian Mounds in Ohio and North Carolina to ruins in India and the former Rhodesia.[2]

0 BC
1000 AD
2000 AD
???
Ancient Metal Working
CHINA

When EVIDENCE is TOO Good

There are several pages within Brilliant which relate not so much to mankind's ingenuity and ability as to his knowledge of dinosaurs. The knowledge and documentation of the co-existence of man and dinosaurs totally destroys the possibility of evolution being true. According to evolutionary theory, dinosaurs lived 60-240 million years ago and mankind did not even start to appear until at least four million years ago. Thus, if evolution were true, ancient mankind could not possibly have any knowledge of dinosaurs. Furthermore, if mankind did coexist with dinosaurs, then 200 million years of Earth history disappears (almost 1/3 of all evolutionary time needed to explain complex life without God) and the evolutionary house of cards collapses. Therefore, any evidence for the co-existence of man with dinosaurs is just "too good" and has to be denied in order to maintain the belief in evolution. Because of this, the evidence for man and dinosaur coexistence will always be extremely controversial and fiercely opposed. But if the evidence were presented in a court of law, would it establish beyond a reasonable doubt the truth of the matter? That is up to the reader to decide.

The few pages of *Brilliant* dealing with this issue are far from exhaustive but come at the evidence from very different angles to give a brief overview of the evidence. Even though some artifacts are indeed controversial, they have been included in this volume in order to allow the reader an opportunity to view both sides of the controversy. These evidences include images of men and dinosaurs together as shown on burial stones in Peru (page 14), undecayed bone-making cells (osteocytes) found inside a Triceratops horn from Montana (page 22), human and dinosaur footprints discovered together at the Paluxy River in Texas (page 24), and dinosaurs found on pottery from ancient Peru (page 116).

Both Bible-believing creationists and evolutionists

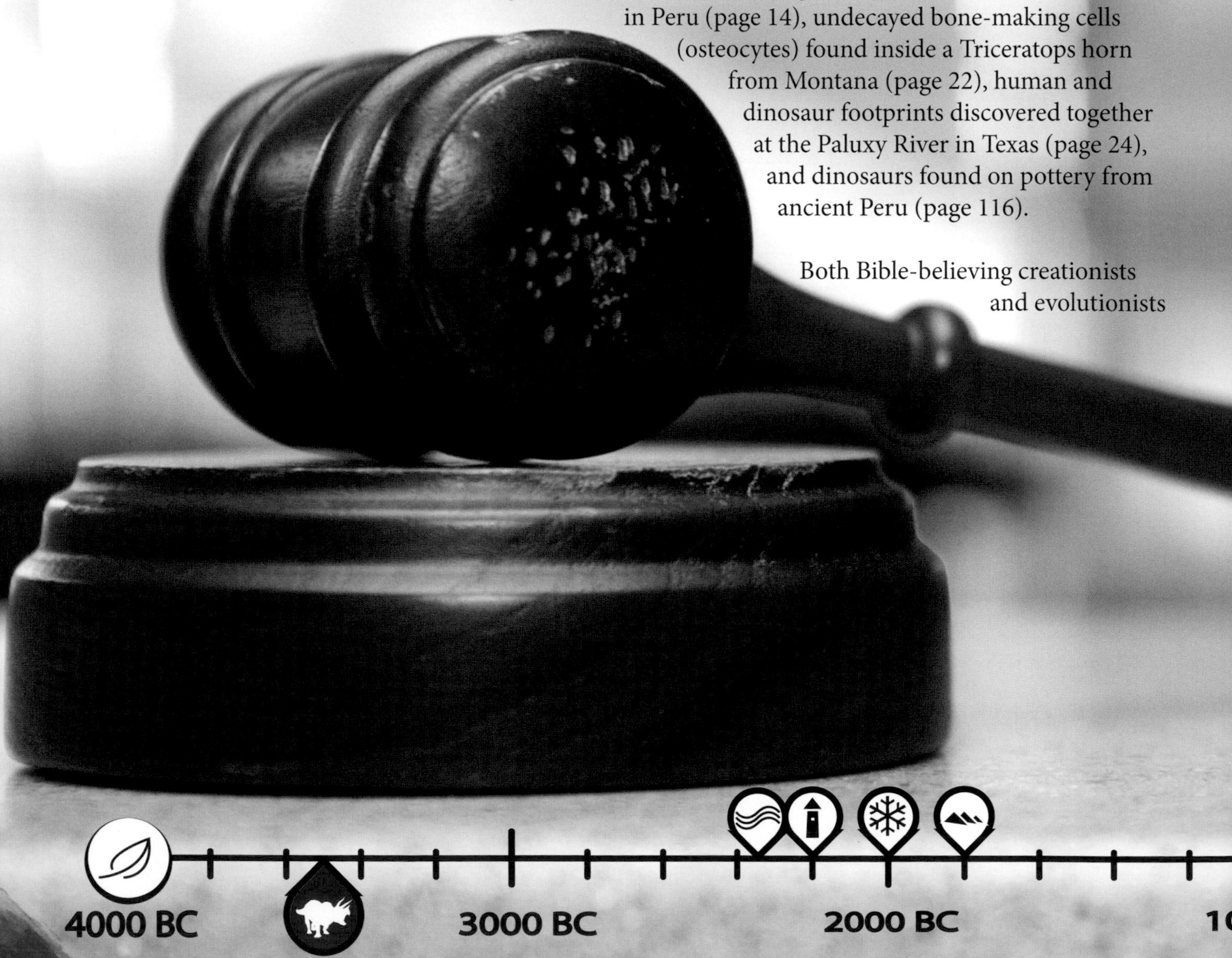

view these types of finds with an extreme bias. Yet those holding to an evolutionary viewpoint have a much stronger and almost blinding motivation to reject such evidence. For the evolutionist, to accept **any** evidence of dinosaur/human co-existence totally destroys the time frame needed for evolution to be true. Thus, the possibility of man/dinosaur co-existence cannot even be considered, and every possible excuse to reject the evidence is accepted and promoted in order to undermine its authenticity. On the other hand, the creation viewpoint can easily continue without any evidence that man and dinosaurs co-existed because that knowledge simply may not have been captured historically or may have been destroyed by the flood. Thus, those approaching the data from a creation perspective understand that the evidence for man and dinosaurs living together fits perfectly into a Biblical perspective (because mankind was created at the same time as all other basic "kinds" of creatures), but they do not need this evidence in order to maintain their belief in creation. In the creation viewpoint, dinosaurs (known as dragons before 1842)[1] could have come through the world-restructuring flood (along with other animals on Noah's ark), and therefore the many evidences for man/dinosaur co-existence from cultures around the world (which arose after the flood) can be accepted as real -- but the Biblical creation viewpoint would not collapse if such evidence did not turn out to be authentic.

An example of how strong this bias can be is recounted by Rick Deighton[2].

In one of Don Patton's seminars he told about an experience he had while doing research on dinosaur tracks and human tracks together at the Paluxy River near Glen Rose, Texas. They had a couple of curiosity seeker guests with them who were not part of the research team. There was a young man in his late teens who was not a Christian, but very interested in the creationism/evolutionism controversy. He was well aware of the reports of fossilized human footprints being found in the same strata of rock as fossilized dinosaur footprints, and the monumental implications of those reports. The other guest with them was an older man who professed to be an honest seeker after truth, but in reality was a committed, dogmatic evolutionist. The evidence of his unwillingness to face factual evidence came out when Don Patton and his team did discover another human footprint fossilized in the same strata of the rock where the dinosaur footprints were found. Don pointed out the track to the younger man, who promptly put his own bare foot into the impression and said, "It's the same size as my foot!" Don also invited the older man to come observe the human track, but that man turned the other way and refused to even look at the track! Why would anyone refuse to look at what he professed to be seeking? Because it would blow the lid off his assumptions and biases. It would destroy his worldview. By refusing to even look he could say, "I didn't see any human footprints." In contrast, the young man was convinced by the evidence and became a believer [in the accuracy of the Bible and Christ as his Savior].

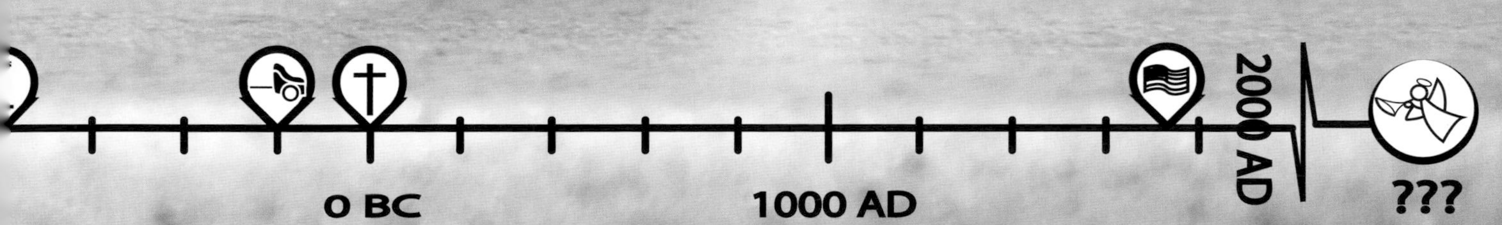

FRESH MEAT
Undecayed Dinosaur Tissue

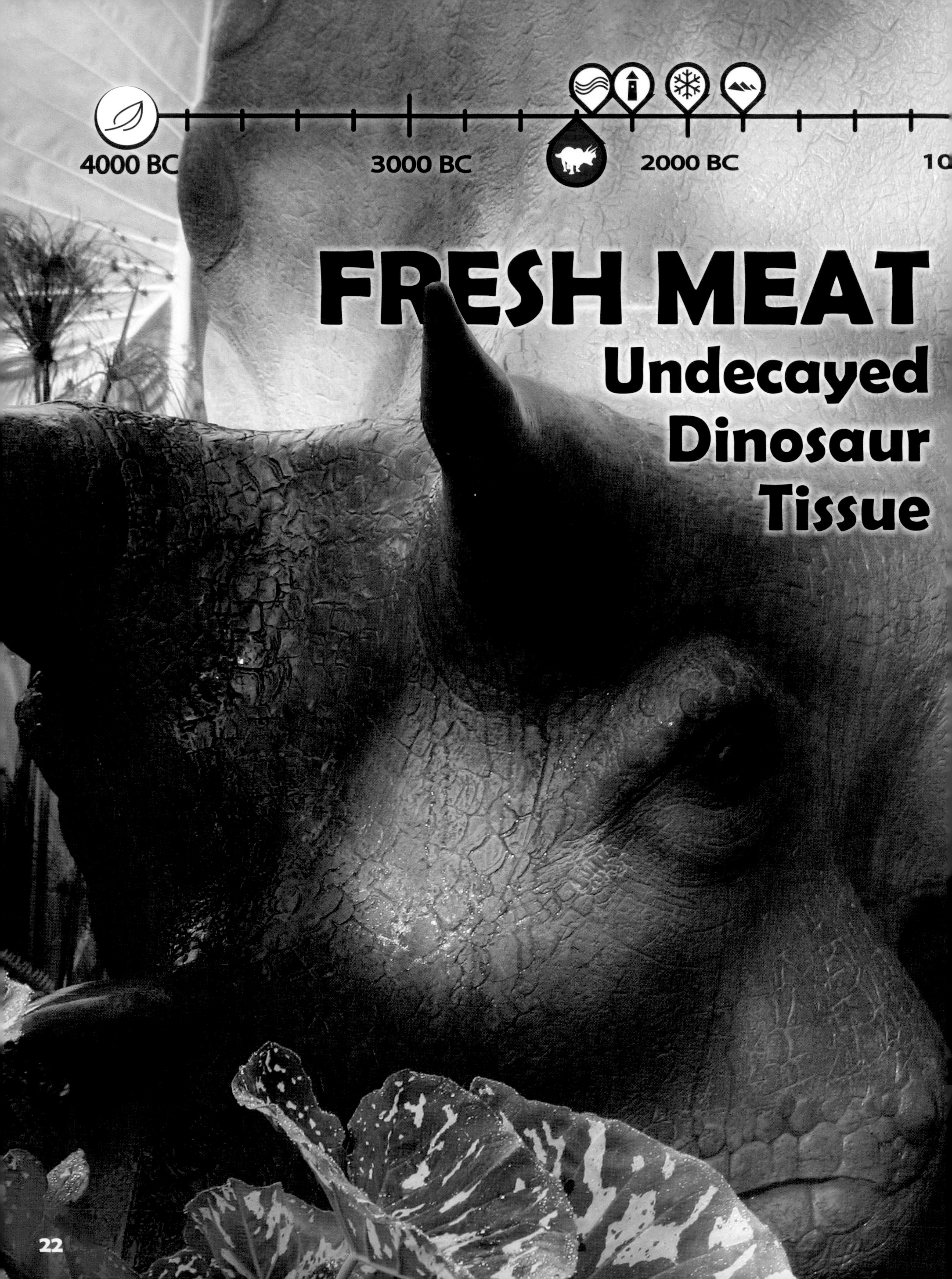

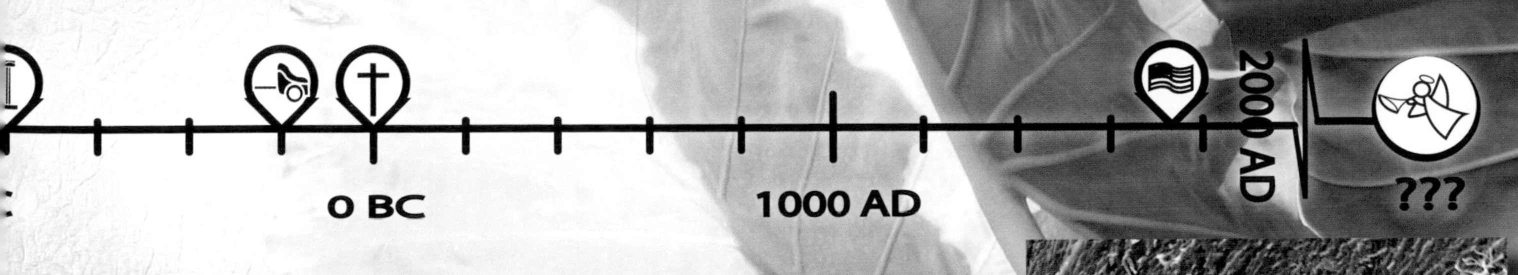

Soft unfossilized tissue continues to be found in a wide variety of fossilized dinosaur remains. The implications of this are apparent to almost everyone. Finding soft tissue inside a fossilized bone means that the bone cannot be millions of years old or else the soft tissue would be long gone. The reason these tissues exist is because dinosaur bones are found in sediment which was buried and rapidly fossilized during Noah's flood approximately 4300 years ago – not millions of years ago. One of the latest finds is a stretchy film membrane containing unfossilized osteocytes (bone-making cells) found inside a triceratops horn.[1] These unfossilized tissues are made of fragile protein molecules, which under the best conditions, (in the absence of water and at low temperatures) have total degeneration projected at less than 30,000 years. So how could the rock layers containing these soft tissues be millions of years old? They could not be!

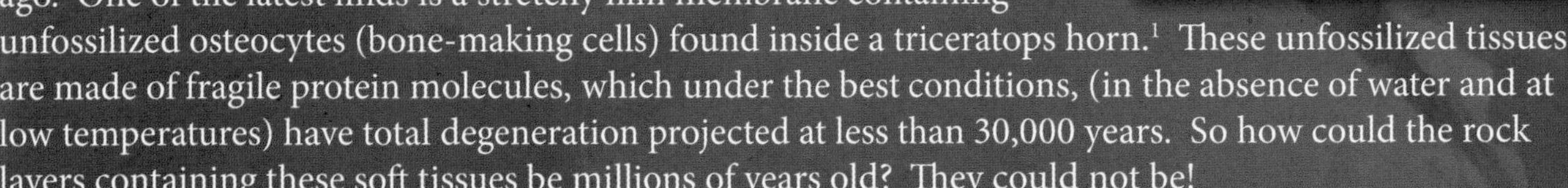

Any medical student in the world would immediately be able to identify these cells as bone-building osteocyte cells. Osteocytes build a calcium structure which link cell to cell, thereby creating an extremely light, yet extremely strong, sponge-like network to structurally support the rest of a vertebrate's body. So how do evolutionists hang onto the belief that such unfossilized material could be around if dinosaurs were, indeed, buried over 60 million years ago? They have proposed that perhaps a modern animal such as a bird, died next to the buried fossil and osteocyte cells somehow migrated out of the bird bones and into the triceratops horn! It seems any story, no matter how far-fetched, is preferable to accepting what the evidence indicates – the recent and rapid burial of dinosaurs and essentially all other creatures in the fossil record.

Mark Armitage, the discoverer of osteocytes in the triceratops horn, and instructor at a microscopy lab at California State University, Northridge, California, showed his students images of the fresh dinosaur tissue. They returned to their Earth science departments excited to share the inconsistency of these finds, (which contradicted the evolutionary teaching they were being taught) with their geology, anthropology, and paleontology professors. The result - Armitage was fired from his job within days of his paper being published in July of 2013. This was in spite of years of stellar performance and excellent reviews setting up and running the university's microscopy lab. It would appear anything goes within state-run universities - except showing students evidence which exposes the hypocrisy and poor science surrounding evolutionary dogma.

Evidence such as this does not relate directly to mankind's brilliance and ingenuity, but it does testify to mankind's knowledge of, and interaction with, creatures which were supposedly extinct millions of years before mankind appeared. This reality totally destroys any possibility of the belief in evolution and its required millions-of-years time frame for the history of humanity.

Evolution Viewpoint (Attack on evidence)	**Creation Viewpoint** (Defense of evidence)
The finder of the fossil is not credible, the location of the find was not documented, and why would he keep the dinosaur print secret for eight years before selling it? How could he have not seen the human foot until ready to sell the print?	The rock contains other fossils testifying to its age and the find location was documented. Museums often find additional discoveries upon closer examination. He just got busy and never cleaned it up until he was ready to sell it -- his story is reasonable.
The prints are way too clear and obvious – they have to be fake.	The line of reasoning is circular – it rejects the evidence because of the implications, not the evidence.
The prints have all kinds of mistakes – big toe too deep, next 3 toes too long and at awkward angle, the middle dinosaur digit is too long compared to other prints, etc.	There are enormous variations in both dinosaurs and humans, so none of this is reason for outright rejection. Similar human impressions have been discovered.
The strongest evidence for the authenticity of the fossil impression is claimed to be the CT Scan slices of the print showing compression under the prints. These are invalid because the scan was done in a medical lab instead of using a more powerful scanner in a controlled university environment. Although the scans show compression around and under the prints, there are inconsistencies and the possibility of false imaging and misinterpretations.	The fact that compression is present proves the prints were not carved or faked. The inconsistencies of where the compression would take place have been explained, and the offer is open for anyone who can guarantee the safety of the artifact to do nondestructive testing as long as unbiased access to ALL of the test results are made available and the owners or representatives are allowed to accompany the fossil.

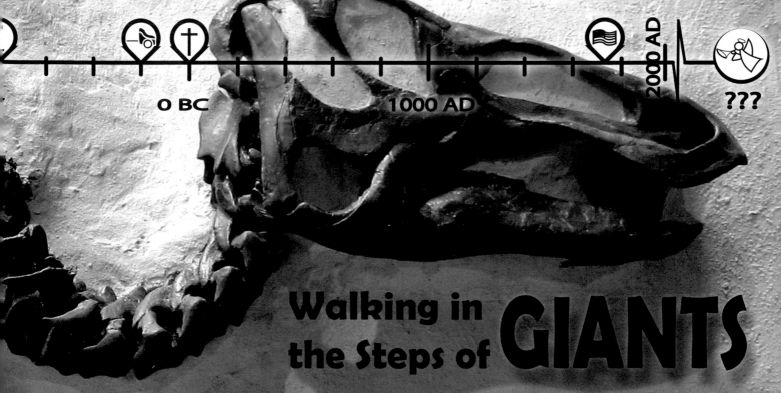

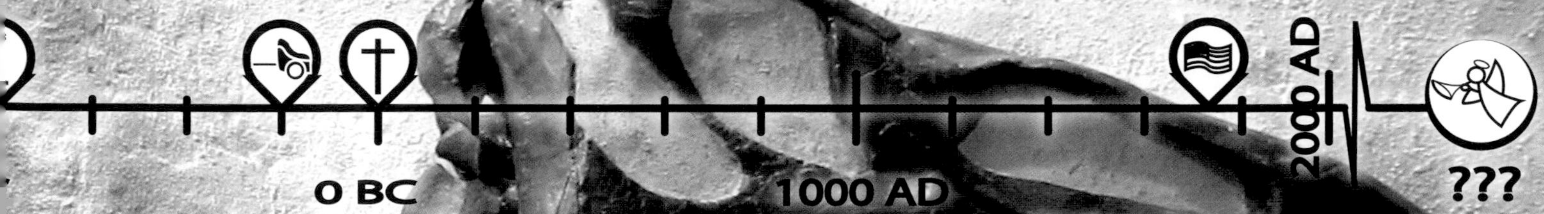

0 BC 1000 AD 2000 AD ???

Walking in the Steps of GIANTS

One of the clearest (and most controversial) artifacts testifying to the reality that man lived with dinosaurs is the Delk print, reportedly found in the Paluxy River area of central Texas in 2000.[1] The jury is still out on whether this startlingly clear print is real or fake, but the response to it from both sides is very enlightening as to how evidence such as this is evaluated. Let's look at the Delk print the same way a jury would look at evidence to determine the guilt or innocence of the accused. Let's pretend in this court case that the belief in evolution is on trial (which cannot have dinosaurs and man living at the same time because this destroys the claim for an enormous age of the Earth) and the Delk print is one of the evidences indicating that evolutionists are misleading others with their belief.

Like any competent defense team, the defenders of evolution approach this find with both barrels blazing and work to cast doubt upon every aspect of the find. Their primary lines of objection are listed in the table to the left, along with the response from those defending this find as authentic.

And that is pretty much where the controversy stands. Evolutionists have nothing to gain and everything to lose by further examination of the artifact. Furthermore, they have no interest in spending time and money studying something their current theory requires them to believe is a fake. Creationists are either wary of the evidence (based on the ferocity of the evolutionary line of attack) or feel nothing further needs to be done to justify its authenticity.

The lesson to be learned from this type of artifact is that all evidence must and will always be interpreted based on the starting assumptions and worldview of the one doing the interpretation. Since all public educational establishments are ruled by the iron fist of naturalistic assumptions, this is the only viewpoint students are allowed to see. Because of this situation, each passing generation contains an increasing proportion of people blinded to any possibility other than evolutionary processes for our origin. This artifact, whether real or fake, is presented here not as a blanket endorsement of its authenticity, but to show what is typical of the discussion which can take place when both viewpoints are examined. Sadly, this seldom happens within our university classrooms when the subject involves evidence surrounding our origin.

Dispersion of Humanity

4350 to 4000 Years Ago

This period of world history is characterized by the re-establishing of man's foothold upon the world. Simply put, humanity was struggling to survive. Within a few generations after the flood, mankind was returning to rebellion against God by worshiping creation, crowding together in a single location (instead of spreading across the globe as commanded), and building a tower which may very well have been a pagan "creation-worship." In response, God again acted in love, dividing mankind into distinct groups by creating different spoken languages, which slowed the spread of evil and resulted in a dispersion of mankind across the globe. Interestingly, after 4,000 years, mankind has finally succeeded in returning to a common mode of communication – the computer language – which can instantly translate any language into another.

Meanwhile, as the oceans cooled, there was an Ice Age rapidly building sheets of ice in northern and southern latitudes while lowering ocean levels hundreds of feet. People

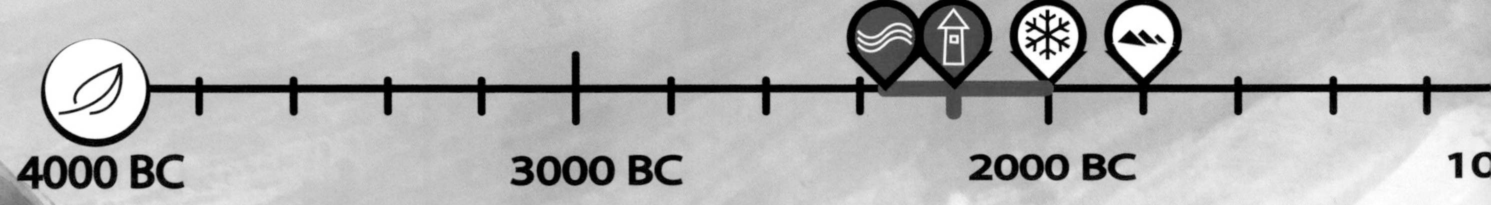

living during this period of Earth history displayed a wide range of skill levels. This variety of abilities and knowledge spanned from primitive to spectacular. At the same time the Egyptians were laying the foundations for pyramids, Neanderthals were gluing rocks to spears in an effort to hunt game in colder northern climates (page 28). While the Chinese were developing a language consisting of 80,000 different characters, Cro-Magnon man was eeking out a living in the caves of frozen France and covering cave walls with paintings which few people today could duplicate in their beauty and complexity (page 30). While the Phoenicians were developing their sailing abilities (no doubt based on knowledge from before the global flood), cities were being built along the shorelines of oceans which were hundreds of feet lower than today's ocean levels – only to be covered with water as oceans rose at the end of the Ice Age (page 40).

To understand this range of ancient abilities and knowledge, imagine our entire world completely pulverized by trillions of tons of sediment-filled water moving across the globe, driven by hurricane-force gales which would dwarf any catastrophic weather event happening today. Energy exceeding millions of atomic bombs would spread around the globe and completely destroy every structure, road, tree, and animal, leaving pulverized, but water-sorted and redistributed, rubble in its wake. Now imagine that you and your immediate family were the only humans to survive this global restructuring and personally had to recreate human civilization based only on the knowledge in your head. How would you recreate electronics, refrigeration, modern construction techniques, flight, combustion engines, etc...? You would start with simple structures, rudimentary tools, stone spears and axes, and probably find shelter in caves. As your descendants continued to spread out, there would be a variety of skill levels as some remembered what you had described to them and would build upon memories of previous technologies, while other branches of humanity (due to infighting or harsher environments) would advance slowly. Mix in a raging Ice Age for the first 500-1000 years, continued reverberations from the flood, and the dispersion of humanity in distinct groupings by language, and you have a pretty good picture of why we find such a variety and diversity of human cultures/abilities developing around the world during this period of human history.

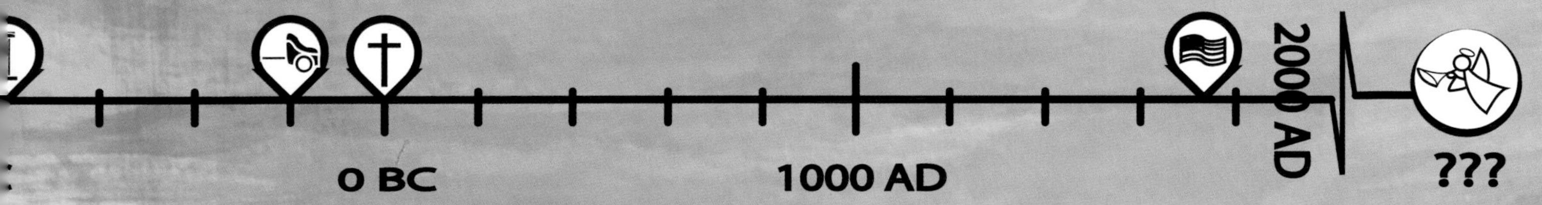

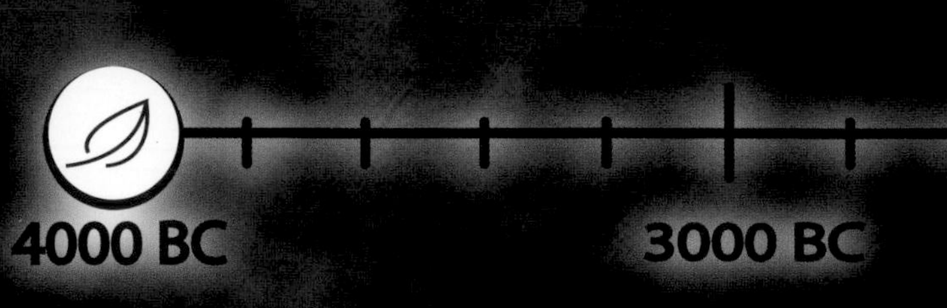

NOT SO DUMB

Neanderthal is portrayed as a knuckle-dragging, wife-beating, dimwitted ignoramus in textbooks, museums, and movies, but recent archeological and scientific discoveries have given him quite an image upgrade.

According to a recent NOVA report, Neanderthals *"had the abilities of modern humans to plan ahead, innovate, and communicate through language, art, and symbolism."*[1] In addition, these people were skilled hunters who used innovative tools, produced articles for purely decorative purposes, and buried loved ones with valuable articles in intricate funerals that included flowers being arranged around the body -- indicating a knowledge that death was not the end of our existence. Neanderthal remains even show evidence of survival to old age despite numerous wounds, broken bones, blindness and disease. This suggests that these individuals were cared for and nurtured by others who showed human compassion.[1] There is also abundant evidence that these people communicated complex issues to each other, meaning they must have possessed complex language abilities. Even more amazing is the recent discovery that these ancient people were able to manufacture chemical glues which modern researchers can only duplicate with great difficulty.

Neanderthals produced durable hunting spears by fitting a flaked stone tip to a wooden shaft and winding animal sinew or fiber cord around the joint. They would then smear what has been characterized as "super-glue" over the binding to make an unbreakable joint. Chemists have discovered that the glue (pitch) used to make this joint can only be produced by heating resinous tree bark (such as birch bark) in an oxygen-free environment at temperatures between 644 – 752°F. If the resin does not reach this temperature, the bark fails to produce any pitch. If the temperature is too high, the resin turns brittle. If oxygen is not excluded, the bark bursts into flames.

In several tests, scientists attempted to reproduce the process by laying bark on a stone surface, covering it with sand to exclude oxygen, and building a fire on top of the sand. However, they admitted that they used a thermometer to regulate the temperature level and only succeeded in making a small amount of resinous pitch over several days of mostly failed attempts.[2]

The fact that modern researchers have a tough time reproducing what men routinely achieved almost 4,000 years ago highlights the superiority of the Biblical viewpoint of man's intelligence. Far from slowly evolving brutish beasts, Neanderthals were merely an intelligent race of people struggling to survive in the frozen fringes of civilization during a raging Ice Age. They exhibited every indication of being innovative, intelligent, and creative. It is doubtful that many people today, thrust into a world where all technology had been destroyed by a worldwide flood, would cope as well.

CAVEMEN

0 BC
1000 AD
2000 AD
???
GERMANY

CAVE ART

Ask people to envision a "caveman artist" and they are likely to describe a slope-headed, long-haired brute scraping the end of a burnt log across a dimly lit wall while dragging his wife by the hair with his other linebacker-sized fist. Why do people have such a poor impression of cave dwellers? Because they have been systematically trained to believe people evolved from some lower form of life – therefore, these ancient ancestors are assumed to be far less intelligent and less talented than modern man. But what does the evidence actually show?

Spread across this page are some of the 2000 paintings found upon the walls of a complex of caves in southwestern France. Eighteen-year-old Marcel Ravidat discovered the Lascaux Cave in the late summer of 1940. He and three friends were the first to view hundreds of animals depicted upon these cave walls. These caves are commonly taught to have been inhabited approximately 17,000 years ago, even though carbon dating of pigment in the drawings places the age of the dwelling at 30,000 years.[1] It is interesting how dates from even well-accepted methods, such as radiocarbon dating, are simply rejected if they do not fit into desired time frames. In actuality, these caves were inhabited by people seeking shelter approximately 4000 years ago - during the Ice Age, which immediately followed the worldwide flood. *[Note: The carbon-14 dating is so wrong because it does not measure a date, just the amount of ^{14}C in the paint pigments. Pigments in the paint made this early in Earth history would have started with far less ^{14}C.]* The cave complex was opened to the public in 1948. By 1955, the carbon dioxide produced by 1200 visitors per day had visibly damaged the paintings and the cave was closed to the public in 1963 in order to preserve the art. Few people today, even with all of our "superior" intelligence and abilities, could produce drawings of such beauty, detail, accuracy, and artistry. Even more interesting is the art at the

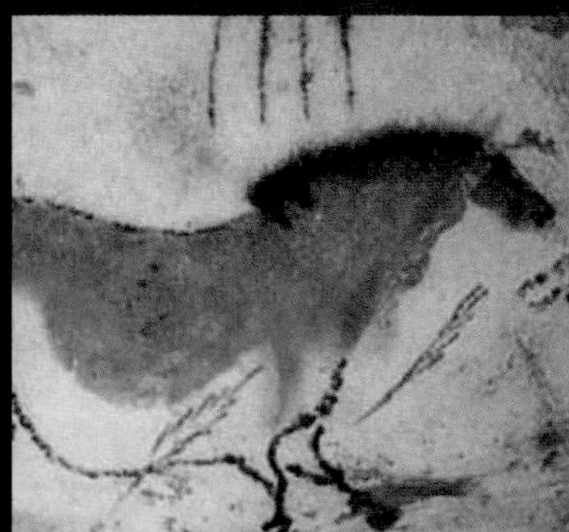

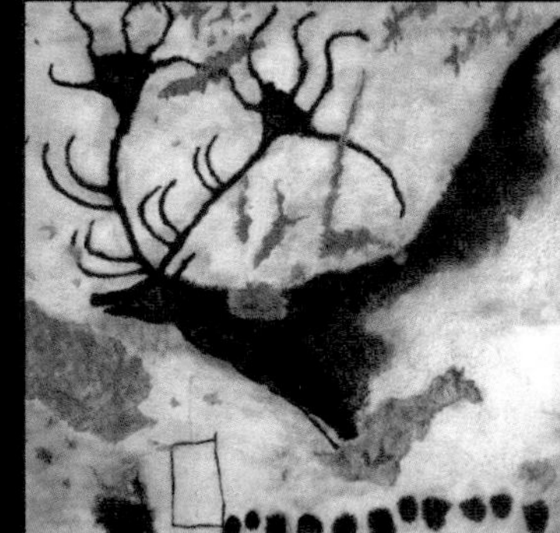

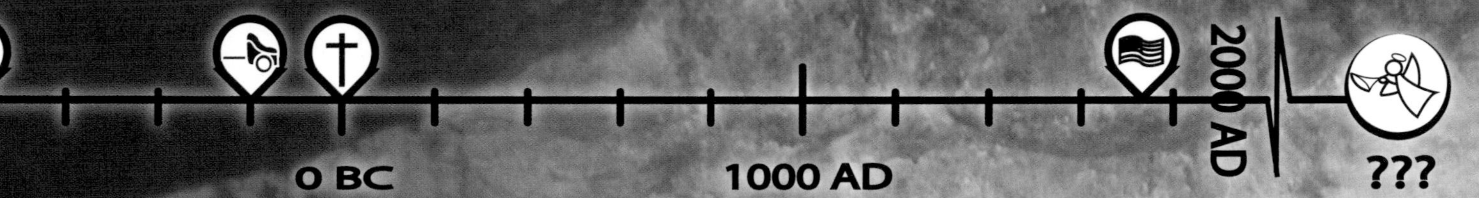

Chauvet cave in southern France. Initially these spectacular representations of dozens of different animals were believed to be much more recent than the Lascaux cave drawings because they were drawn even more intricately – thus they were considered more highly "evolved" art. It turns out that the opposite is true – they are now listed as twice the age of the Lascaux art – showing that the more ancient people were actually more, not less, skilled! In actuality, both of these caves were probably painted during the Ice Age period, within hundreds of years of each other, about 4000 years ago. Both caves are now open only to researchers (only a few hours each month), and scientists are still struggling to preserve the artwork from relentlessly encroaching mold.

In addition to being artistically talented, the people who made these drawings were keen observers of nature. By comparing the pictures drawn of horses with actual photographs taken of horses in full gallop, it is clear that most of these and other ancient cave drawings correctly show the running gallop of a horse, which even many modern painters fail to capture correctly. These direct descendants of Noah showed both incredible artistic talent and observational abilities that few people today could match. The cave drawings are hardly the unsophisticated doodling of a low-IQ half-ape in the process of becoming fully human. Once again the evidence fits perfectly into what would be expected from a Biblical model of history while straining the credibility of what would be expected from an evolutionary view of mankind.

4000 BC

3000 BC

BC

THE ORIGINAL MEGA CHURCH

The oldest worship center on Earth has been unearthed less than 400 miles from Mt. Ararat.

It has long been assumed by archeologists that mankind ("hunter-gatherers") slowly evolved a belief in God as an explanation for the things they observed as they developed a greater and greater awareness of the world around them. Thus it was only when they were more fully "evolved" that they started to develop formal religious beliefs and traditions. But in the words of Ian Hodder of Stanford University, *"Göbekli Tepe changes everything"*.[1]

Göbekli Tepe is the site of an ancient ruin which German archeologist Klaus Schmidt started uncovering in 1995. Although he has explored less than five percent of the ancient ruins (the area is approximately 50 feet high and 1000 feet in diameter), what he has uncovered has astounded the archeological community. The hill is known to contain more than 200 limestone pillars, with the larger ones standing 20 feet tall, weighing as much as 40,000 pounds, and capped with horizontal stones. These huge monolithic structures are covered with intricate carvings of lions, bulls, boars, foxes, snakes, insects, vultures, gazelles, and a multitude of symbols of unknown creatures. Some of them even have three-dimensional animals carved from the solid limestone. The pillars are arranged in multiple circular patterns, and it is estimated that 500 people would have been required to quarry and move each stone from pits located up to 1/3 mile from the site. Furthermore, there is an abundance of butchered animal remains found at the site, but no evidence of human remains in the lower levels – indicating that this was not a burial site or village but an early worship center.[2]

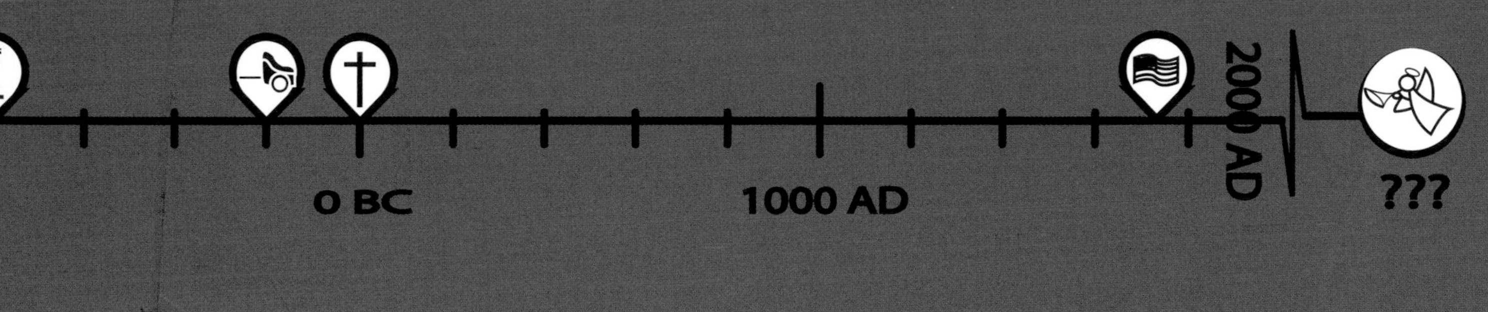

It is no coincidence that one of the first acts of Noah after coming off the Ark was to set up an altar in order to offer a sacrifice to God (Genesis 8:20). As humanity multiplied, both during and after the building of the Tower of Babel, this practice no doubt continued. It is quite likely that this ancient archeological dig is the location of just one such worship location where pilgrims traveled for miles in order to gather in worship of their Creator after the flood of Noah. The massive structures of this complex are hardly the work of ignorant hunter-gatherers who were struggling to survive. The site is obviously the product of a highly intelligent humanity which was working to reestablish the buildings and structures like which they had been told about from before the flood.

The entire region was also lushly forested during this wetter period of Earth history. This is completely consistent with the wetter worldwide climate which would have existed during the Ice Age immediately followed the flood of Noah. Carbon dating of artifacts places the age of the site at 10,000 –12,000 years. However, remember that carbon dating does not tell the age of objects, only the amount of radioactive carbon left. Everything else is an assumption. Because Göbekli Tepe was built shortly after the flood, there would have been very low levels of radiocarbon in things that existed at this time compared to the amount of radiocarbon in things alive today. (See page 42.) It is interesting to note that the artifacts in the caves of France were dated significantly older (i.e. 17,000 – 32,000 years); yet the creators of that art must have lived only shortly earlier in history than those building the complex at Göbekli Tepe. This is because the atmosphere's carbon-14 level was rapidly increasing after the flood. Cro-Magnon man and Neanderthal man were people living in caves in France and Germany during the colder Ice Age, approximately 4200 years ago, whereas the people of Göbekli Tepe were inhabiting a warmer region of Turkey as little as 100 - 200 years later; yet their starting radiocarbon levels were significantly different, so they are misinterpreted as having lived during vastly separated time periods.

Everything about Göbekli Tepe fits perfectly with what would be expected from people and the environment within a few hundred years after the flood. From the low carbon-14 levels to the lush forestation during the Earth's wetter Ice Age period, from the huge size of the monuments to the intricate and artistic carvings throughout the complex; it is obvious that mankind's rebuilding after the flood was done by people of great skill and intelligence.

TURKEY

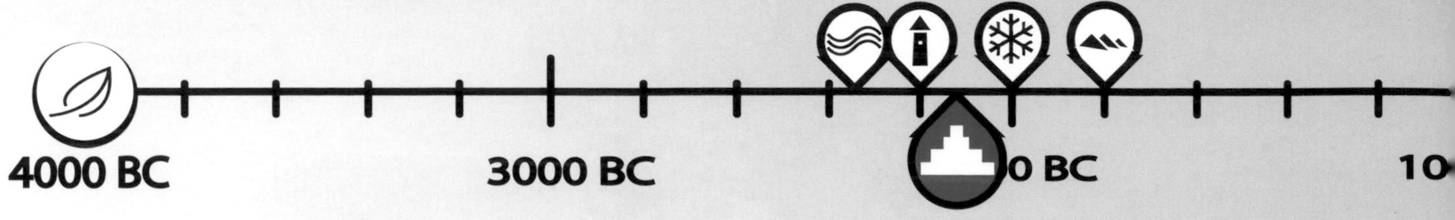

POST FLOOD CITIES

Archeologists routinely point to four great civilizations from which all major cultures of the world developed. North and South American cultures are believed to have been direct offshoots from these other civilizations:

1. The Egyptians
2. People from the Mesopotamia area around the Tigris-Euphrates river system (Abraham, along with major civilizations such as the Assyrians, Babylonians, and Persians, came from this area.)
3. The Chinese
4. The Indus Civilization

Much has been written about the technology and abilities of the first three, but little attention is typically given to the last. Yet this people group may have been the largest one to separate at the Tower of Babel and the most prolific of the ancient city-building civilizations. Even today the descendants of the Indus civilization (people living in India and Pakistan) are the largest people group on earth, exceeding even China's estimated population of 1.36 billion.

The extremely sophisticated cities of Mohenjo Daro (Mound of the Dead) and Harappa have been discovered in the Indus Valley of modern-day Pakistan. Discoveries of these cities have forced archeologists to push the dates for the origin of Indian Civilization back thousands of years. At its peak, the Indus Civilization is estimated to have had well over five million people skilled in architecture, metallurgy, and art. Over 1,000 settlements have been identified, of which less than 10% have been excavated.[1]

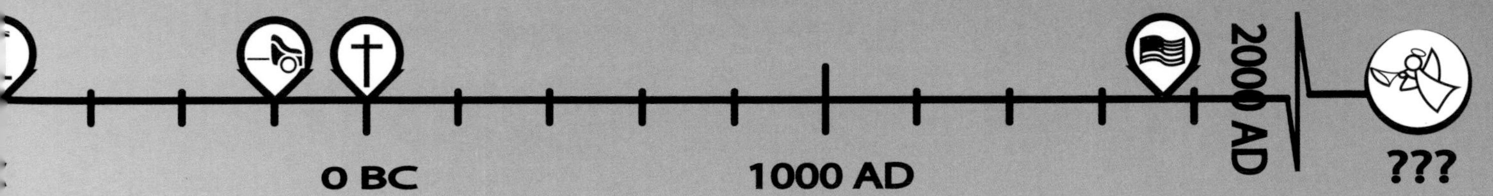

This vast, well planned city-building civilization sprang up from just one of the language-family groups which spread out from the Tower of Babel approximately 4200 years ago. It is the speed and skill with which these people developed what were essentially modern cities - with baked brick buildings, huge community bath houses, and city-wide sanitation systems - which astounds researchers. Plumbing-sewage systems run throughout the large cities in a way superior to that found in Pakistan, India, and most Asian countries today. Some of the larger homes for the wealthier citizens include rooms that appear to have been set aside for bathing, and at least one residence has been unearthed which had an underground furnace believed to have been used for heated bathing!

So what happened to this advanced civilization? As with most ancient cultures[2,3], it was likely a degeneration of morality which led to the decay and ultimate collapse of the culture and, with this collapse, the loss of knowledge and technology. Greed, cruelty, brutality, slavery, sexual immorality, war, apathy, dishonesty and corruption will ultimately destroy any society which rejects an absolute moral foundation from outside their own laws. If morality is a matter of human opinion, then the most powerful (or ruthless) people will rise into a position of control and simply change the moral standards to suit their own sinful desires. Ultimately society implodes, and with it is lost the order, organization, and technology achieved by the original society. We ignore this lesson from the past at our own peril.

PAKISTAN

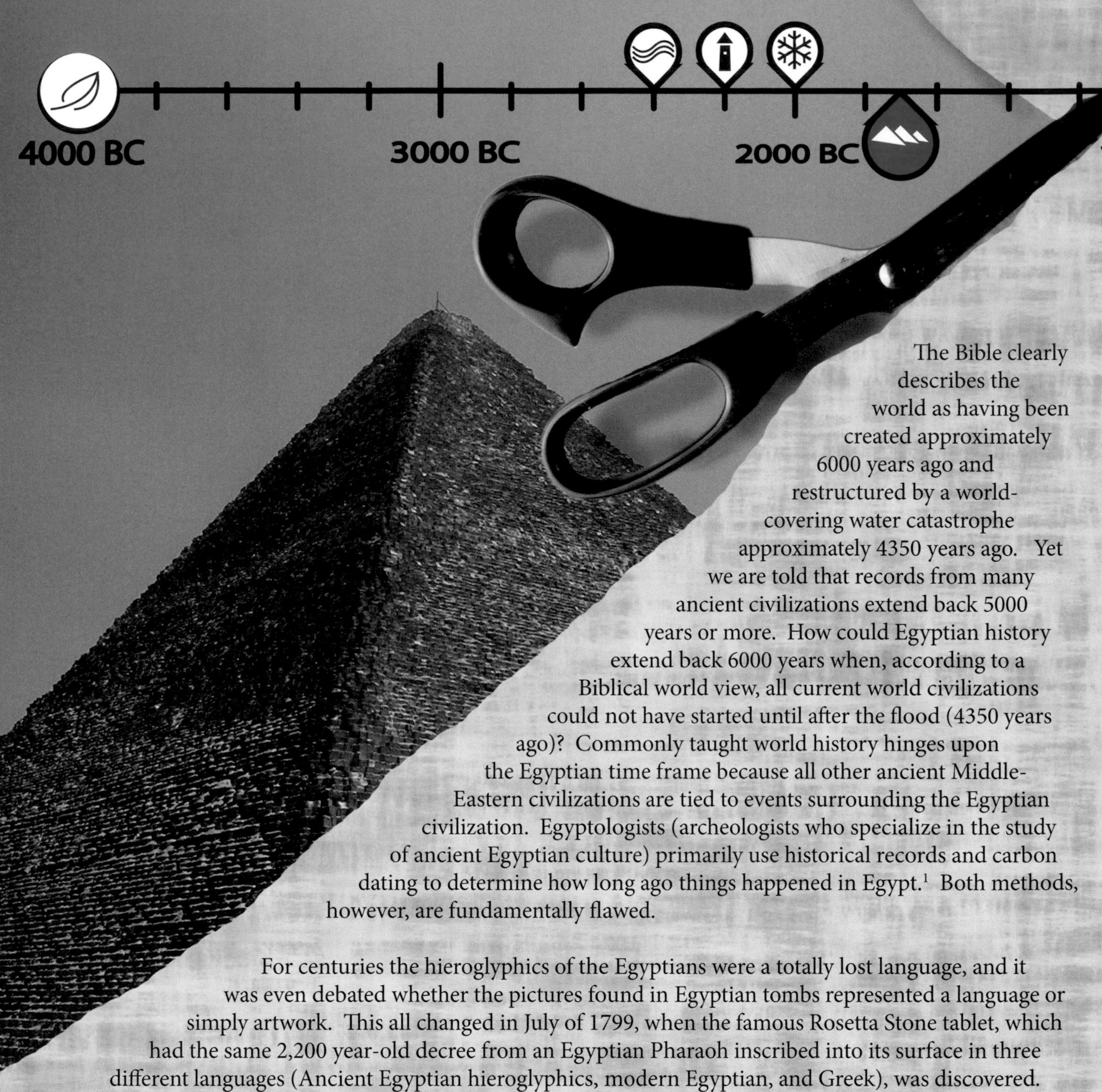

The Bible clearly describes the world as having been created approximately 6000 years ago and restructured by a world-covering water catastrophe approximately 4350 years ago. Yet we are told that records from many ancient civilizations extend back 5000 years or more. How could Egyptian history extend back 6000 years when, according to a Biblical world view, all current world civilizations could not have started until after the flood (4350 years ago)? Commonly taught world history hinges upon the Egyptian time frame because all other ancient Middle-Eastern civilizations are tied to events surrounding the Egyptian civilization. Egyptologists (archeologists who specialize in the study of ancient Egyptian culture) primarily use historical records and carbon dating to determine how long ago things happened in Egypt.[1] Both methods, however, are fundamentally flawed.

For centuries the hieroglyphics of the Egyptians were a totally lost language, and it was even debated whether the pictures found in Egyptian tombs represented a language or simply artwork. This all changed in July of 1799, when the famous Rosetta Stone tablet, which had the same 2,200 year-old decree from an Egyptian Pharaoh inscribed into its surface in three different languages (Ancient Egyptian hieroglyphics, modern Egyptian, and Greek), was discovered. This single document became the key to unlocking ancient hieroglyphics. The original Rosetta Stone is the most visited display in the British Museum of London, England. Using the Rosetta Stone as a key to the Ancient Egyptian language, palace records from the first Pharaoh of Egypt (commonly referred to as "The First Egyptian Dynasty") through the fall of Egypt were translated in the 1800s - revealing an unbroken span of almost 9000 years of Egyptian history. Yet no Egyptologist still believes the royal records of the ancient Egyptians can be taken at face value to reveal that much time for the Egyptian civilization.[2] Three sources of error are now acknowledged:

1) Northern kingdom and Southern kingdom pharaohs often both claimed to be rulers of the entire region even though they ruled different regions at the same time. Thus, the length of their dynasties cannot be added together because they were taking place simultaneously.

2) The total length of the reign of many pharaohs has been found to be exaggerated to make rulers appear more powerful. In other words, the royal scribes lied to make their kings look more god-like. Thus, the

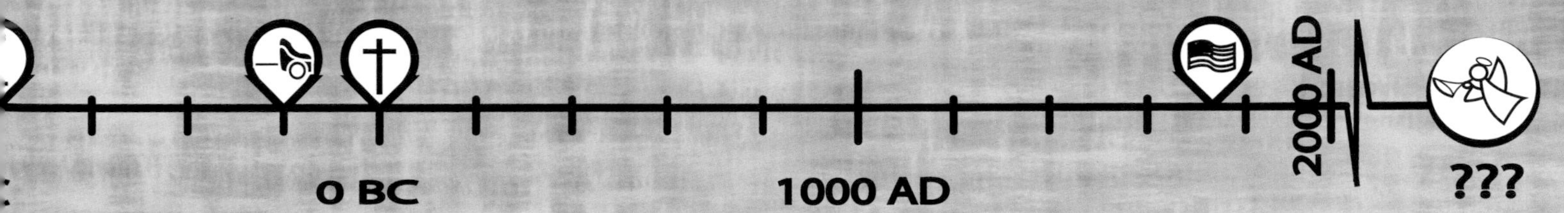

Cutting History Down to Size:
The True Egyptian Timeline

9000 year-old Egyptian civilization (taught as a fact in the 1800s) has been downgraded by most experts to be the 6000 year-old civilization taught today. The question remains – how do we KNOW this age is true?

3) All carbon-14 (^{14}C) dates are based on the assumption that we know how much radioactive carbon was in the tissue of the things when they were still alive. Yet there is extensive evidence that before and shortly after the flood the entire biosphere of the Earth would have had a far lower ^{14}C concentration. This dating method does not directly measure the age of an object – it just measures how much ^{14}C is left and assumes that a "small" amount means an "old" object. Yet if the sample contained less ^{14}C to begin with, it is not very old - it is just from a time period in the past when less ^{14}C was available.[3]

Here is a probable timeline tying Biblical and "commonly taught" history together. There is actually no valid scientific or archeological reason to reject the Biblical timeline. Note that even Bible scholars are still arguing about whether the ancient Masoretic or Septuagint texts is the more accurate, so these dates are just approximate based on the most widely accepted Masoretic Bible dates.[4] Using the Septuagint text would actually add about 700 years to the time available for cultures to have formed after the flood. Comparing the Biblical timeline to secular history, this difference is trivial. In *Brilliant* we will consider whether the more recent Masoretic date for the flood - approximately 4350 years ago - is even possible.

4,150 years ago - The first people arrived in the Nile Valley after dispersing from the Tower of Babel.

3,900 years ago - Abraham came to Egypt during The First Egyptian Dynasty, pretending Sarah was his sister.[4]

3,700 years ago - Joseph was sold into Egypt, rising in stature to the god-like vizier named Imhotep during the Third Egyptian Dynasty. This historical Egyptian figure was second in command only to pharaoh and was responsible for many major building projects and a massive increase of wealth in the nation.

3,450 years ago - Moses rose to power and the Old Egyptian Dynasty collapsed due to plagues and Hebrew slaves leaving Egypt. Amenemhat IV of the Sixth Dynasty of the Old Kingdom (this corresponds to the Second Dynasty of the Middle Kingdom – the Old Kingdom and the Middle Kingdom actually overlap and run parallel) dies without leaving a successor.[5]

For years the Bible has been considered non-credible to those studying ancient history because they have extended the Egyptian timeline too far into the past and therefore failed to see that key events in Egyptian history (the collapse of the "Old Dynasty" and other events) exactly correspond with the biblical narrative of Abraham, Joseph, Moses, and their exodus from Egypt. By correcting the Egyptian timeline, a true understanding of ancient history is restored, and all other key events in ancient history immediately correspond to the Biblical narrative.

The Real Population Explosion

According to the most widely accepted ancient Bible texts, the worldwide flood happened approximately 4,350 years ago and Abraham arrived in Egypt approximately 3900 years ago. Other ancient world civilizations (Phoenicians, Mayans, Chinese, etc.) also seem to have started developing advanced civilizations about 4000 years ago. There are several logical questions concerning these dates: When was the Tower of Babel, which resulted in the dispersion of distinctly different people groups across the globe? How could eight people coming off the Ark have resulted in such widespread and advanced civilizations so rapidly? To answer these questions one must examine how quickly the human population likely increased following the flood of Noah.

Let's start by making several logical assumptions:

A. Early in human history people were far healthier and lived longer for three primary reasons:

1. Genetic mistakes within human bodies were not nearly as widespread because every subsequent generation adds its own set of genetic mistakes to the growing number previously placed upon the DNA code. More genetic mistakes result in each subsequent generation having slightly more medical problems.
2. The Earth's magnetic field has been documented to have decreased by fifteen percent in the last 150 years. Extrapolated backwards, this corresponds to doubling the Earth's magnetic field approximately every 1000 years. Therefore, 4400 years ago the Earth's magnetic field could have been almost twenty times stronger – greatly increasing the protection provided from harmful solar radiation.
3. Far fewer harmful bacteria and viruses would have been in existence because these, too, are constantly mutating and changing – creating new diseases over time.

B. Siblings intermarried freely:

Ancient cultures commonly allowed marriage between close relations. Marriage of siblings and cousins was not restricted until 1000 years after the flood (at the time of Moses) because by then so many cell duplication mistakes had built up that sexual union between close relations resulted in almost certain birth defects.

C. The average family size was likely twenty or more children:

In recent years the largest number of children born to a single woman is over forty. There are dozens of documented examples of women having twenty or more children.[1] People after the flood lived longer and would have been highly motivated to have extremely large families. Even if the average family was only ten, a shorter twenty-five-year generation time would yield essentially the same results.

Using very conservative assumptions, let's see how fast the human population would have increased:

- If Shem, Ham, and Japheth (Noah's sons) each had 20 children within 50 years of the flood, there would have been 30 child-bearing couples on the planet within 50 years of this event.

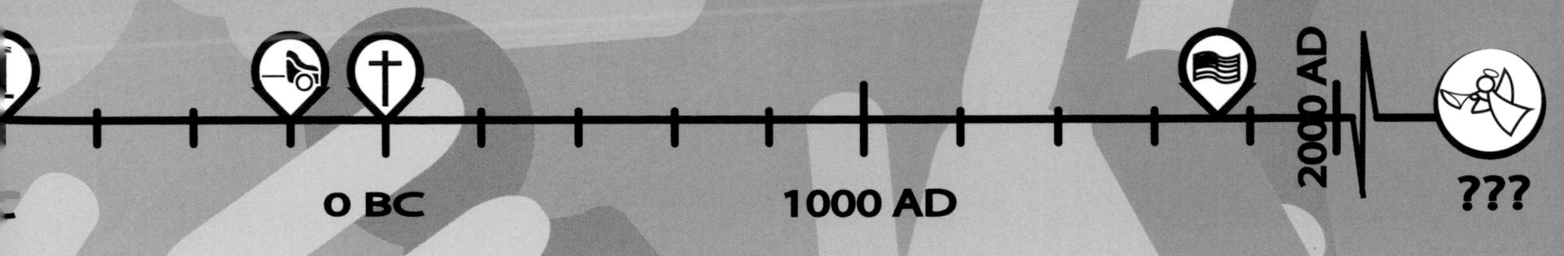

- If these 30 couples each had 20 children, within 100 years of the flood there would have been 30 x 20 = 600/2 = 300 child-bearing couples on the planet.
- If these 300 couples each had 20 children, within 150 years after the flood there would have been 300 x 20 = 6000/2 = 3000 child-bearing couples on the planet, etc...
- By 200 years after the flood the population of the Earth could have been 30,000 couples (plus all the people born since the flood who were no longer having children) which equals about 66,000 people.

Let's assume the Tower of Babel was built 200 years after the flood. (No one knows the exact date.) At this point humanity was broken up into many distinct linguistic groups. Let's assume seventy. This means each group traveling outward from the Tower of Babel would have started out with approximately 950 people (428 couples of child-bearing age). If one of these people groups arrived in Egypt around 4150 years ago, let's see how many people could have been in this region at about the time Abraham traveled there, 3900 years ago:

- After another 50 years there could be (428 x 20)/2 = 4280 couples.
- After 100 years there could be (4,280 x 20)/2 = 42,800 couples.
- After 150 years there could be (42,800 x 20)/2 = 428,000 couples.
- After 200 years there could be (428,000 x 20)/2 = 4,280,000 couples.
- By the time Abraham visited Egypt 3,900 years ago (250 years after the dispersion of humanity at Babel), the number of people who had settled in Egypt alone could have been in excess of 80,000,000 people!

By this time human cruelty/sin would have again started to take its toll and families may have started to have far fewer children, so that likely there were not nearly so many people living in early Egypt -- but this illustrates how there was plenty of time from the flood of 4,350 years ago for a highly advanced, structured, pyramid-building civilization to have developed before Abraham visited the country 3900 years ago (in approximately 1900 BC).

What doesn't compute is how the Egyptian culture could be thousands of years older than the Bible indicates without leaving evidence for billions of people having inhabited this fertile area of the world over those thousands of "missing years." Archeologists generally agree that the early ancient Egypt area was inhabited by somewhere between one to ten million people. (Estimates vary widely.)[2] This relatively small number of people living in a lush, fertile river valley area makes perfect sense if the Biblical timeline is accurate, but no sense if the Egyptian culture is thousands of years older than the Biblical timeline would indicate.

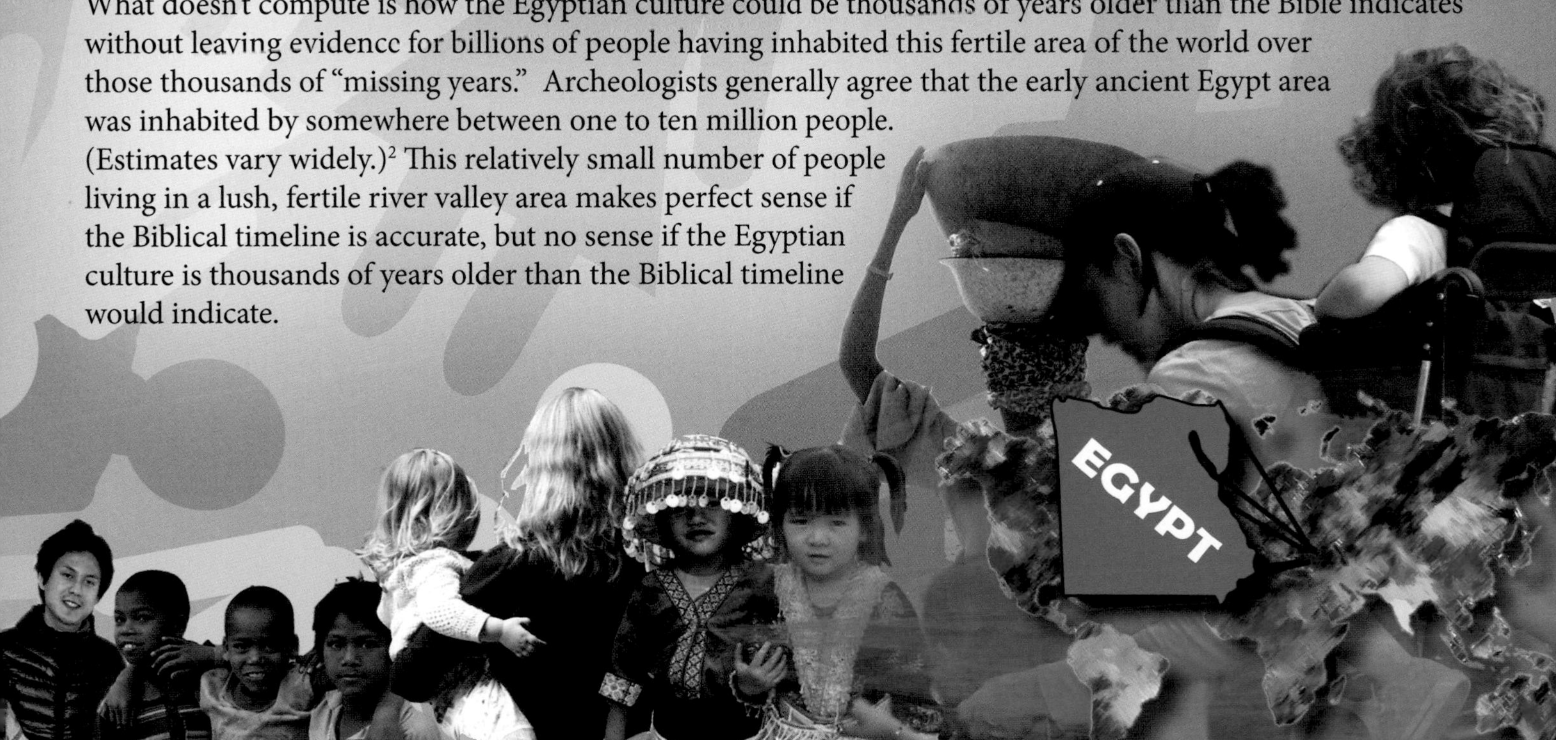

ICE CITIES

After the worldwide flood of Noah's time the oceans of the world were left significantly warmer than today due to massive land movement and volcanism during the flood. These warmer oceans resulted in massive evaporation which condensed as snow – covering northern and southern latitudes with sheets of ice thousands of feet deep. This event immediately followed the flood and resulted in a lowering of ocean levels for hundreds of years following Noah's flood. All scientists acknowledge that during the last Ice Age the oceans of the world were 200 to 300 feet lower than today. They just get the date wrong, misinterpreting the Ice Age – by assuming it started 200,000 years ago and ended 10,000 years ago. So where does the Ice Age fit into biblical history?

The Ice Age and the building of the Tower of Babel followed rapidly after the global flood and people were migrating around the globe while accumulating ice was lowering worldwide ocean levels. People spreading around the globe mapped newly formed land surfaces and built cities and civilizations wherever they traveled. It is both logical and natural that many of these ancient cities would have been located adjacent to the ocean. However, hundreds of years after the dispersion from Babel, the oceans of the world cooled to a new equilibrium temperature (today's oceans have an average water temperature less than 40°F), water evaporation slowed from the ocean's surface, and the enormous sheets of ice began to **rapidly melt** – causing a catastrophic and rapid rise in ocean water levels.

Think about the enormous concern and propaganda surrounding "climate change" and the possibility that enough ice at our polar caps would melt to raise ocean levels 2 to 3 feet. This is a drop in the bucket compared to what happened 3600-3800 years ago when the ocean levels rose 300 feet - covering entire coastal cities within a few generations. This is also the likely origin of the legend of Atlantis – supposedly covered by waters of the Atlantic Ocean as the ancient civilization sank into the sea. In reality, Atlantis didn't sink…the sea level rose to cover this and many other coastal cities.

Where is there evidence for these lost cities? Under the water along the coast of many nations! The map at the bottom of this page shows the known locations of undersea structures around the world. Many of these structures are badly eroded because they have been under the sea for almost 4000 years, yet they definitely seem to be the remains of huge man-made cities. The structures are controversial because they cannot be adequately explained unless the ocean levels rose rapidly approximately 3800 years ago at the close of the

Ice Age (which followed the worldwide flood). Yet Earth Science textbooks incorrectly place the end of the Ice Age at 10,000 or more years ago – long before mankind had built any major city-like structures. These cities can be found along the coastlines of Egypt, Malta, India, and Japan.[1]

The evidence fits perfectly into a Biblical perspective of Earth history, but causes controversy and mystery for those clinging to an ancient Earth perspective. Highly advanced civilizations building cities along the ocean 3600 – 4000 years ago only to abandon these massive stone structures as the ocean levels rose at the end of the Ice Age, fits seamlessly with an Ice Age starting 4200 years ago and ending 3600 years ago but makes no sense if the Ice Age ended 10,000 years ago. By denying Biblical truth, modern archeologists are forced to either:

(1) attribute these underwater structures to recent earth quakes dropping entire cities into the ocean (there is no evidence for this and it had to have happened with out destroying the structures);
(2) believe that Stone Age brutes building enormous cities (which also does not fit the unintelligent ancient man paradigm);
(3) calling these ancient cities "natural rock formations" (in spite of the obvious evidence to the contrary).

Only the Bible provides the key to solving such mysteries of the past. By placing evidence into a biblical timeframe of Earth history, many such historical mysteries disappear.

Rebuilding of Civilization

4000 to 3000 Years Ago

People were busy exploring and populating the world throughout this period. Areas from North America to Australia are filled with fascinating artifacts from distinct people groups, which developed their own linguistic, physical, social, and cultural distinctives -- due in large part to early isolation from other people groups. War, greed, prejudice, and distrust kept cultures largely separated and prevented much of the knowledge and technology developed in one culture from being shared with another. Furthermore, technological advances seem to have popped up in one culture, only to disappear without further advancement in another culture as one group of people enslaved and annihilated another.

Historians mischaracterize this period of Earth history more than any other, due to the misinterpretation of two things – the timing of the Ice Age and a misunderstanding of carbon dating. Thus, terms such as "Stone-Age" and "Bronze-Age" are commonly attached to time frames of 30,000 – 3000 years ago, and these time frames are taught as if they are a fact of science. After the dispersion from Babel, there was rapid development of cultures throughout the world, with extremely advanced civilizations arising in Egypt, the Mediterranean, China, and South America. But during this same period there was an Ice Age raging across the Earth. Although

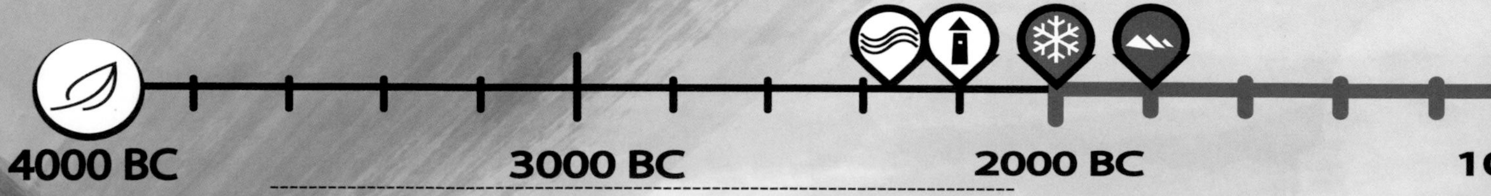

the ice covered only northern and southern latitudes, it had enormous worldwide implications on population migration, and during the winding-down stages of the Ice Age there would have been many advances/melt-backs of the ice sheets -- which have been misinterpreted as multiple ice ages throughout time.

The timing of the Ice Age is THE KEY for archeologists and anthropologists as they speculate on the timing of all pre-Egyptian civilizations. But since they do not start with the acknowledgement of a real, world-restructuring flood (that heated the world's oceans and initiated the Ice Age), they misplace the date of the Ice Age at 200,000 – 10,000 years ago. Thus, they are forced to believe that the development of civilizations started over 10,000 years ago, when in reality civilizations rapidly redeveloped around the world starting about 4000 years ago.

A misunderstanding of carbon dating adds to this confusion. Unstable carbon-14 (^{14}C) is produced by sunlight in our upper atmosphere by a process of radiation from the sun colliding with atoms in the atmosphere and forming neutrons, some of which collide with nitrogen atoms. This collision forms the very rare, one-in-a-trillion, carbon-14 atoms in the atmosphere. The result is a uniform concentration of this unstable form of carbon in every living organism. This unstable ^{14}C starts to disappear upon death and one-half disappears approximately every 5000 years (rounded down for simplicity). Thus, if an old bone or spear shaft is found, and it has 1/16 of the carbon-14 found in things alive today, it is assumed to have been alive 20,000 years ago (the original amount divided in half 4 times = 1/16th; each division taking 5000 years = 20,000 years). But lost upon most researchers is the reality that what is being measured is not time -- it is simply the amount of ^{14}C within an artifact. The starting amount of ^{14}C in living organisms before the flood would have been much lower than today. For instance, before the flood, the Earth was a paradise with far higher numbers of organisms and plants than are in existence today. Therefore, even if the ^{14}C generation rate was the same before the flood as it is today, the amount of ^{14}C could have been 1/10th the modern level - even while an organism was still alive. Thus, when a low level of ^{14}C is measured, it does not prove that the artifact is extremely old, because it simply started with less ^{14}C. In addition, current measurements reveal that the magnetic field of the Earth is decreasing by one-half approximately every 1000 years. During the flood this field would have dropped even faster as the Earth's magnetic field rapidly reversed.[1] Thus, the Earth's magnetic field could easily have been 20 times (or more) stronger before the flood, resulting in less solar radiation reaching our atmosphere and far less ^{14}C being generated.

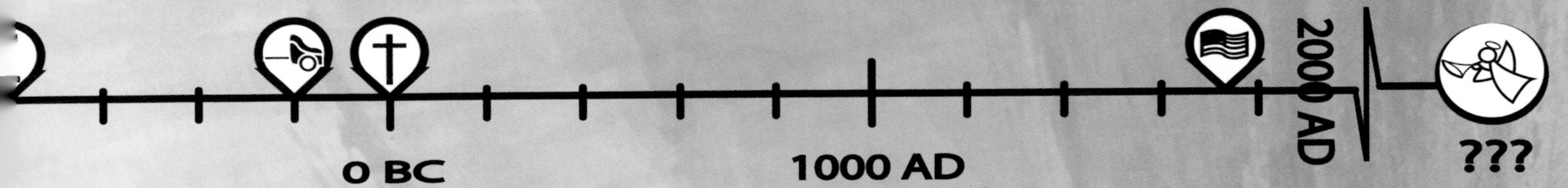

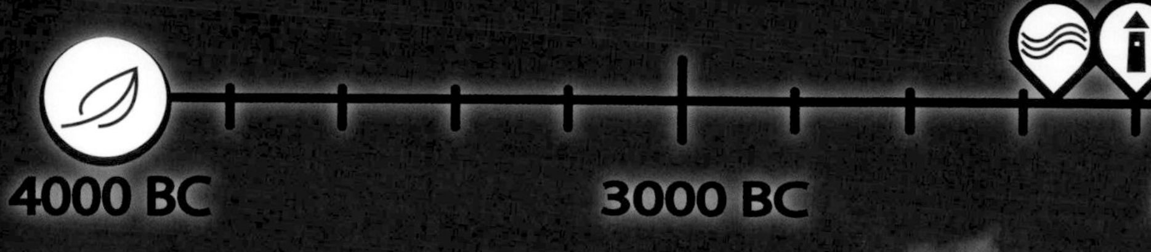

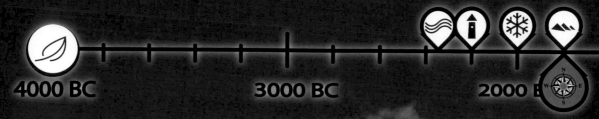

Mapping the Past

In 1929, a group of historians found an amazing map on gazelle skin. Subsequent research showed that it was a genuine document drawn in 1513 by Piri Reis, a famous admiral of the Turkish fleet in the 16th century, whose passion was cartography. Reis' high rank within the Turkish navy allowed him to have privileged access to the Imperial Library of Constantinople. The Turkish admiral admits, in a series of notes on the map, that he compiled and copied the data from at least twenty other source maps, some of which cite materials going back as far as the Library of Alexandria in the fourth century BC (or earlier). What makes this map so remarkable is the accurate portrayal of the coast of Antarctica (which is currently covered with a permanent ice sheet over 5000 feet thick). The shape of this coastline was not accurately determined until seismic mapping of the underlying coastline was performed in 1949. So how could the Piri Reis map reproduce this coastline using sources from 2,300 or more years earlier?

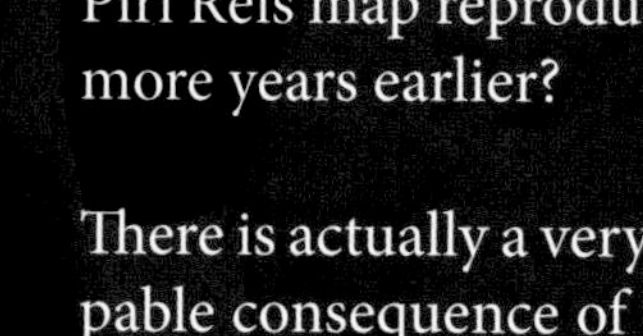

There is actually a very logical and simple explanation. An unstoppable consequence of the global flood of 4350 years ago was massive heat input to the oceans of the world from "the fountains of the great deep," volcanism, underwater lava flows, and rapid movements of the Earth's continental plates. It would have taken many centuries for the oceans of the world to cool. While the ocean water was still very warm there would have been significantly increased evaporation, a wetter climate worldwide, and immense ice buildup in the polar regions as the evaporated ocean water came down as snow. Yet near the Antarctic coastline the ice would not have built up for centuries -- until the oceans cooled sufficiently for the water to freeze over. Interestingly, one of the notes on the Reis map states that the Antarctic region had a "temperate climate." Today, temperatures range from 10°F to -50°F. There would have been plenty of time for seafaring peoples after the flood to have explored, mapped, and reported on this area before it became permanently ice-covered. Furthermore, during the Ice Age, ocean levels worldwide were lowered as much as 300 feet, making the coastline slightly different than we observe today. It is the map's notation of a slightly different coastline and a warmer climate near the coast which make it such a remarkable confirmation of Biblical reality. Ironically, the primary objection to the map's authenticity are these specific observations: *"[Part of the Antarctic coastline] is shown hundreds of miles north of its proper location and the Drake Passage is completely missing, with the Antarctic Peninsula presumably conflated with the Argentine coast. The identification of this area of the map with the frigid Antarctic coast is also difficult to reconcile with the notes on the map which describe the region as having a* **warm climate.**"[1]

Yet these same "problems" are what confirm the map's authenticity! As with almost every piece of evidence which does not fit into the enormous-age paradigm of modern education, anomalies such as the Piri Reis map are simply ignored, denied, or rejected by those blinded by the assumptions of the evolutionary time scale.

Past researchers, less blinded by evolution's time frame, were more honest in evaluation of evidence. Such is the case with the evaluation of the Piri Reis map by Prof. Charles H. Hapgood of Keene College. He specifically requested cartography experts in the U.S. Air Force to evaluate the part of the map corresponding to the coastline of Antarctica (currently covered with ice). This was the Air Force colonel's response (my emphasis added):[2]

TO: Prof. Charles H. Hapgood, Keene College
Dear Professor Hapgood,

Your request of evaluation of certain unusual features of the Piri Reis Antarctica map of 1513 by this organization has been reviewed. The claim that the lower part of the map portrays the Princess Martha Coast of Queen Maud Land, Antarctica, and the Palmer Peninsula, is reasonable. ***We find that this is the most logical and in all probability the correct interpretation of the map.*** *The geographical detail shown in the lower part of the map agrees very remarkably with the results of the seismic profile made across the top of the ice-cap by the Swedish-British Antarctic Expedition of 1949.* ***This indicates the coastline had been mapped before it was covered by the ice-cap.*** *The map shows this part of Antarctica ice free. The ice-cap in this region is now about a mile thick. We have no idea how the data on this map can be reconciled with the supposed state of geographical knowledge in 1513.*
-Harold Z. Ohlmeyer, Lt. Colonel, USAF Commander

It may be prudent to accept the evaluation of U.S. Air Force experts over the "group-consensus-managed" opinions of Wikipedia and other modern evaluators of the map. Any modern interpreter puts his credibility and academic advancement at risk should he admit that the Antarctic region was explored and mapped during the height of the Ice Age (3,800 years ago). Yet this is exactly what the map shows, and this evidence fits perfectly into a Biblical understanding of Earth history.

In 200 BC, ancient Greek historians compiled a list of the seven greatest wonders of mankind's building ingenuity. Of the items on this list, the 100-foot tall Colossus of Rhodes statue, the 400-foot-tall lighthouse of Alexandria, the Hanging Gardens of Babylon, and the Ephesus Temple of Artemis were all destroyed by earthquakes or fires. The only remaining structure from this ancient list - still intact almost 4,000 years after its original construction - is the Great Pyramid of Giza. For over 3600 years the Great Pyramid held the record as the tallest manmade structure on Earth - standing 480 feet tall. The structure was also originally covered with sloped, polished white casing stones - making it a brilliant landmark, visible from over twenty-five miles away. Most of these casing stones have long since been plundered for use in other Egyptian structures, but the underlying, stepped pyramid has survived to this day.

Built as the tomb for Fourth Egyptian Dynasty Pharaoh Khufu, the entire structure was obviously planned by an architectural genius, with intricate interior passageways leading both up and down into three separate burial chambers.[1] Significantly, this is among the oldest of the Egyptian pryramids but it is also the largest, most intricately designed, and the most finely crafted. No slow gradual evolution of abilities is displayed. Later pyramids actually exhibit a deterioration of craftsmanship and size. The perfect, almost airtight, placement of the stone blocks, the planning and forethought needed to design the interior chambers and passageways, and the alignment of the structure all testify to the incredible genius of the designer. No other structure ever built by mankind has withstood the ravages of time this well. The pyramids have been the subject of awe, wonder, and speculation for thousands of years as the mystery of their construction continues to this day.

The magnitude of this project is mind-boggling. The stones were produced from precisely cut 5,000 to 160,000 pound blocks of limestone and marble, which were quarried and transported from locations up to 500 miles away. The Great Pyramid was constructed using an estimated **5 billion** pounds of rock and the construction was believed to have taken fewer than twenty years, using a peak work crew of 40,000. But even this testifies to the enormous intelligence of these people. The Great Pyramid is estimated to contain 2.3 million individual, precisely cut blocks. Working ten hours a day, 365 days a year, for twenty non-stop years would require a block to be precisely placed into the structure every two minutes! Even modern building techniques do not achieve this level of activity.

Even more amazing than the size of the project is the perfect location and alignment of the structure. The Great Pyramid's north-south axis is aligned to within three-sixtieths of a degree of true north-south. It is noteworthy that this alignment is more accurate than that of the Meridian Building at the Greenwich Observatory in London, which deviates from true north by nine-sixtieths of a degree.[2] This could not have happened by accident and indicates an advanced understanding of the builders of the shape, size, and coordinate locations of the Earth. Using advanced compasses and all of modern man's scientific instrumentation and abilities, the modern Greenwich observatory is sixty-six percent less accurate in measuring the Earth's true north-south alignment than people 3600 years earlier were able to achieve! Obviously, mankind's intelligence was there from the very foundations of civilization.

0 BC
1000 AD
2000 AD
???
Dying with Distinction
EGYPT

Bosnia

Pyramid Copycats

One structure seems to show up repeatedly in civilizations which are so old that essentially nothing remains of these cultures – except their massive building projects. That structure is the pyramid.

When one thinks of pyramids, one naturally envisions Egypt. But the same-shaped structure has been found in other locations throughout the world. Amazingly, these other locations reveal man-made pyramids even larger and older than those found in Egypt. Yet modern archeologists are so blinded by the assumption that ancient mankind was less developed than modern man that these ancient structures are routinely misinterpreted as natural hills rather than sculpted pyramids. A perfect example is located just outside of Visoko, Bosnia (near Sarajevo). This pyramid structure was sculpted from the earth of an existing hill and stands 720 feet tall (fifty percent taller than the Great Pyramid of Giza), with the four distinct sides perfectly aligned with the cardinal compass directions of North, South, East and West.

Long since covered with soil, the entire structure seems to have an underlying cement-like, stone conglomerate layer about three feet under the current soil layer - which prevents local citizens from digging cellars under their homes. In many places where this layer has been uncovered, it forms perfect rectangular patterns which have not been explained by any natural process, but look very much like poured or cut blocks covering the sloped surfaces. More evidence for the non-natural origin of the structure comes from the fact that smaller pyramid-hill structures in the immediate area form a perfect equilateral triangle from their apices. Man-made, stone-lined tunnels have also been excavated near the complex.[1]

The amount of earth which had to be moved to sculpt these pyramid-shaped hills is mind-boggling. For an ancient people to then cover the enormous pyramid structure with rock agglomerate or shaped stones amounting to 2.6 million cubic meters of rock, is an undertaking of almost unimaginable proportions. No wonder archeologists, who assume ancient man was unsophisticated and ignorant, cannot bring themselves

Peru

0 BC

1000 AD

2000 AD

???

China (from satellite)

to accept the overwhelming evidence that these structures were built by ancient, intelligent people. If this pyramid isn't enough to convince experts of the brilliance and industry of ancient man, look no further than the pyramids that have been found in Shaanxi in the province of Xi'an, China. One of these pyramids is twice as tall and twenty times the volume of the Great Pyramid of Egypt! Once again, this pyramid is aligned perfectly with the north/south and east/west compass directions, is made from sculpted earth, and was covered with giant stones – most of which have been removed for other purposes. Satellite pictures of the area reveal an entire complex of sixteen or more smaller pyramids. Ancient Chinese records simply refer to these structures as "old" - meaning their construction predates any historical Chinese records.[2]

Enormous mounds sculpted into ancient pyramid-type structures have also been identified in Ohio, Japan[3], and Caral, Peru. In addition, the Aztecs of Central America and the Mayans of Mexico built pyramid-type structures for use as sacrificial temples.[4] Why did so many ancient cultures - starting with those that predate all modern civilizations (3,500 - 4,000 years ago) - keep producing this same pyramid-type structure?

An understanding of Biblical history provides a simple and logical answer. After the Tower of Babel, people spread out in distinct groups all over the world. They took with them knowledge and skills from before the flood. As previously shown (page 38), within a few hundred years any one of these groups could have grown to a population exceeding a million people – fully capable of undertaking massive construction endeavors. Apparently one of their many skills was the building of pyramid-type structures used in the worship of creation. Or perhaps building on high ground gave comfort to those whose forefathers had recently experienced a world-covering flood. This pyramid-building continued wherever people traveled and flourished. Thus, we find evidence of this knowledge from a common source spread throughout cultures around the world.

MAYAN

The Mayan culture was started by dispersed people from the Tower of Babel as they gained footholds in various locations throughout North and South America. The Mayan culture was renowned for its architectural, astronomical, and mathematical achievements. For instance, the Mayans calculated the exact time required for the Earth to travel around the sun as 365.2420 days. The modern value has only been placed at 365.2422 days within the last 100 years, and the Mayan value is actually more accurate than the number used by the modern Gregorian calendar. The accuracy to which the Mayan measured the Earth's passage around the sun is within +/- 8 seconds of the 31,556,926 seconds in a given year.[1] It is unknown how they achieved such accuracy and why the accomplishment was not repeated by any other culture for thousands of years.

It is also significant to note that the very earliest Mayan settlements are dated to around 3,800 years ago (called the "Preclassic Period"). The earliest Mayan settlements were agricultural, growing crops such as corn, beans, and squash. According to official archeological sites, "The Preclassic Mayans also displayed more advanced cultural traits like pyramid-building, city construction and the inscribing of stone monuments."[1] In other words, at essentially the same time that the Egyptians were building their great pyramid projects, the Mayans were also building pyramids and inscribing them with hieroglyphic-type writings. Since both cultures separated from the builders of the Tower of Babel only generations earlier, does this come as any surprise?

4000 BC

3000 BC

2000 BC

MATHEMATICS

There are two other amazing bits of knowledge displayed by these ancient people:

- First was the use of "zero" in their calendar manipulations. The use of zero as a numerical placeholder allowed them to manipulate extremely large calendar numbers into the hundreds of millions of digits. Although credited to the Mayans as early as 2100 years ago, it was quite likely used much earlier. Europeans did not start to use zero in their mathematical calculations until 1500 years ago.
- Second is the Mayan understanding of the origin of time. The Mayan calendar placed the creation of humanity at about 5100 years ago. A straightforward reading of Genesis places the date of creation closer to 6000 years ago, but the similarity is strikingly close. Why would they have picked a number so close to the Biblical number unless they had a common source of information (knowledge which came to them via their common ancestor - Noah)?

Sadly, distortion of the truth increased with the passage of time to the point that during the peak of their civilization, the Mayans were routinely worshiping the sun, considered creation as eternal and our world's current age only the latest in an eternal cycle of creation recreating itself. They also practiced gruesome human sacrifices, which make today's horror films mild by comparison. Is it little wonder God allowed their culture to collapse and disappear?

MEXICO

BC

1000 AD

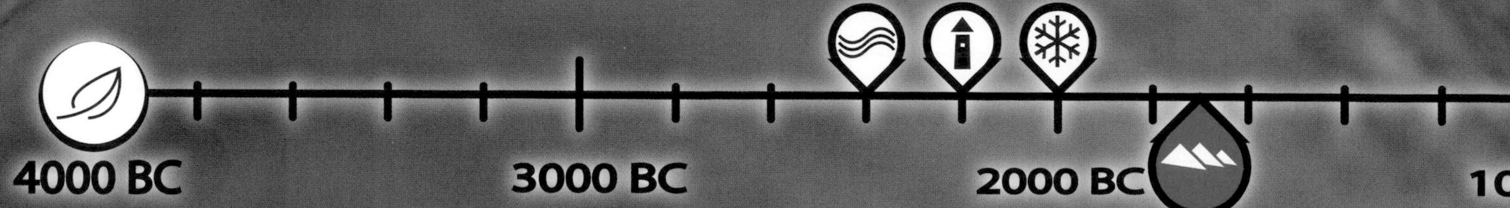

Egypt's Iron Age

Archeologists build their perceptions of the past based on what they have been taught by those who preceded them. It has been the overwhelming consensus that mankind's discovery and use of materials for tools has slowly developed over time. The "three-age system" created by Christian Thomsen (1788–1865) has been locked into the minds of historians for over 150 years.[1] In this classification system, primitive mankind used stone tools from 12,000 - 5000 years ago (the "Stone Age"), learned to make copper tools from 5000 - 3300 years ago (the "Bronze Age"), and discovered how to produce and use iron from 3300 - modern era (the "Iron Age"). In addition to the totally wrong dates in this human-invented classification system, man's use of iron has been irrefutably documented all the way back to ancient Egypt, over 4000 years ago. In the British Museum is a piece of wrought iron that was discovered in 1837 between the joints of the ancient limestone masonry of the Great Pyramid.[2] For what other purpose might this metal have been used?

There are many mysteries surrounding ancient Egyptian artifacts which are generally ignored because these people are classified as ignorant humans caught between the "Stone Age" and the "Bronze Age." Nothing could be further from the truth. In addition to the accuracy of the alignment of the Great Pyramid (page 46), the accuracy with which they were able to cut the individual stones is mind-boggling. In 1883 Sir William Matthew Flinders Petrie made meticulous measurements of the remaining casing stones which covered the Great Pyramid.[2] His measurements, complete with statistical error bars, is still available for analysis. He showed that the casing stones, many as large as twelve feet long and weighing 40,000 pounds, were cut to a total length variation averaging less than +/- 0.020 inch.[3] This is unheard of, even with today's cutting technology, and is impossible for individual hand-hewn rocks.

The mystery deepens as other ancient Egyptian artifacts are examined. Vases and other objects made from marble and extremely hard granite have spiral cutting marks on their interior. The background of this page

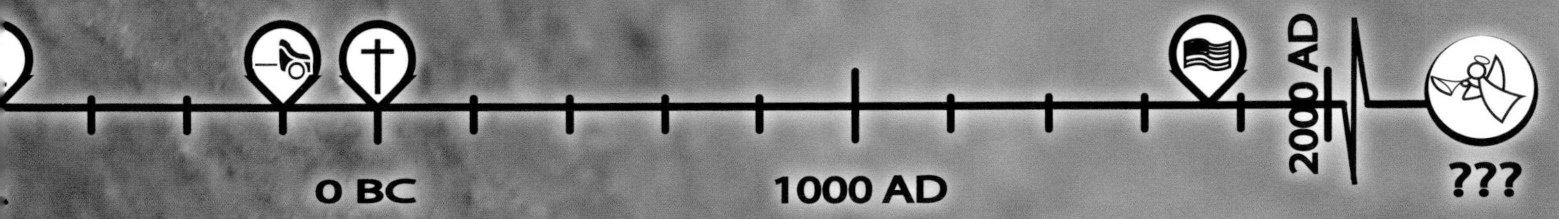

is a photograph of the inside of such a vase, which obviously shows those circular grooves. As a revolving circular cutting saw is forced down into a stone surface, it can efficiently cut a circular opening into stone if constantly supplied with highly abrasive hard-grit slurry at the cutting surface. However, a very accurate method of revolving the steel tool at high speeds with tremendous pressure would be required. More intriguing is the fact that as the tool descends, it leaves circular marks, indicating the rate at which it is drilling deeper into the stone with each revolution. Modern stone cutting tools typically drill down at 0.0002 inches per revolution, but the Egyptian artifacts show a drilling rate of 0.1 inches per revolution – 500 times faster than modern tooling! Most intriguing is that the drilling rate was faster through harder materials (like quartz) than softer materials (like feldspar). The only method currently known which allows for this faster drilling through harder materials is ultrasonic drilling, which vibrates the crystals in the rock such that they fracture as the drill touches their surface.[4,5]

So what is the bottom line? If the blinders of modern arrogance are removed, this type of evidence points to ancient man having the ability to use high-speed abrasive saws or wire-cutting techniques to cut the stones for the early pyramids, and tubular saw drilling for holes and contours. They also seemed to have combined the drilling techniques with knowledge of ultrasonic or other fracturing technology that has been lost in time. This knowledge apparently came down to them from techniques used before the Flood. So why have such tools not been uncovered in Egyptian archeological digs?

Such advanced technologies may have been one of the many things which gave the Egyptian culture a great advantage over other nations. Both the techniques and expensive tooling were likely highly guarded secrets kept in the royal treasury when not in use. They may not have wished their technological secrets and advantages to be carved upon their monuments. War, economic collapse, social unrest, and a multitude of other issues may have caused the great building projects to diminish, and with them the tooling to fall into disrepair and disuse – the parts being plundered and remelted for other purposes. Only speculation remains, but many of the artifacts constructed by these brilliant people remain to this day.

Beautifying Technology

Historians correctly understand that the Japanese people separated from the Chinese during the Ice Age, migrating to the islands of Japan during this period of Earth history (when ocean levels were lower), and became an isolated/unique people group. Because archeologists ignore the effect of the worldwide flood, they misplace the start of the Japanese culture, putting it at 10,000 years ago instead of realizing that the Ice Age followed the worldwide flood approximately 4,400 years ago, making the Japanese culture much younger.

From their inception, the Japanese have borrowed technology and ideas from neighboring cultures, modified it for their own use, and added beauty to utility. Thinking of Japan invokes images of intricately tiered temples, finely crafted black lacquered woodwork, peaceful gardens, and colorful artwork and clothing. Yet early in their history, survival was the priority.

Immediately after settling on the islands, the Japanese started to modify their environment in order to prosper. The oldest Japanese people were known as the Jōmon. These inventive people excelled at hunting technology -- building seven-foot-deep holes with sharpened sticks at the bottom which killed, bled, and suspended large-game animals that fell into the pits. They carved barbed fish hooks from antlers; produced twelve-foot-long bamboo fishing poles using hair or silk as fishing line; made nets from woven rope, floats from pumice, and sinkers from fired clay; and built underwater weirs (walls) to guide fish into enclosed spaces where they were easily harvested in large numbers. Harpoons have even been found dating back to the very beginning of the Jōmon culture, indicating that these innovative fishermen hunted larger sea creatures such as dolphins, tuna, or perhaps even whales.[1] These advances in providing food for a large population were so successful that the Japanese rapidly spread throughout the islands, and had leisure time for developing other technology and artwork for which they are well known.

Lacquering of wood is a unique Japanese art form which can be traced back almost 4,000 years. Lacquering is a long, difficult

process. First, sap from a lacquer-producing tree must be collected and filtered. Then the correct proportion of various colored pigments or oils is added. The thick, glossy liquid is next spread onto a wood surface and allowed to dry between coats until a thick, perfectly smooth layer is built up with a deep color and rich shine. Metal helmets, swords, and armor were also brightly lacquered such that even the weapons of war became objects of beauty. Japanese woodworking equipment and swords are, to this day, among the most finely crafted in the world.

These early settlers to Japan were also aware of astronomical events as they set up large stone megaliths (similar to Stonehenge in Great Britain) at Kanayama in the mountainous region of central Japan. The monuments are believed to have serve as ancient calendars.

From the very beginnings of civilization the Japanese also excelled at pottery-making. Early pottery used rolled ropes of clay that were wound and smoothed to produce vessels, but even 3,500 years ago they were producing fired clay figurines of intricate beauty, known as *Dōgu.*[2]

The Japanese also understood that there was life after death - burying their ancestors at great expense and effort. Over two millennia ago they were building hundred-foot square and circular mounds with stone-lined burial chambers. Some of these keyhole-shaped burial mounds required the transportation of twenty-six million cubic feet of soil and twenty-eight million pounds of stone. It is estimated that such tombs today would consume seven million man-years of labor, costing $800 million to produce.[3]

The Japanese epitomize the artistic abilities of mankind. Not simply content with surviving, throughout their history they modified writing, woodcarving, landscaping, construction, and clothing – everything they touched was enhanced via attractive artwork and vibrant colors. Being made in the image of God, they brought not just inventiveness and intelligence to their endeavors, but artistry and beauty as well.

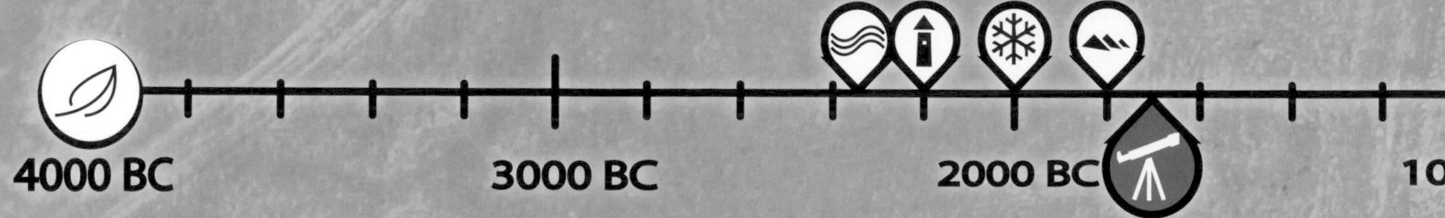

Sight to the Blind

The mindset that ancient people were too ignorant to have developed optics has blinded modern researchers to the obvious evidence right in front of their eyes. Hundreds of finely ground optical lenses from ancient cultures have been found. But because these artifacts do not fit the widely disseminated story of evolution, they are either denied to be actual lenses made from polished transparent quartz crystals or assumed to be modern fakes. Yet extensive evidence from a multitude of ancient cultures testifies to the fact that they did indeed manufacture and use optical lenses.[1]

Robert Temple spent a lifetime studying this issue and writes, "*The eyes of ancient Egyptian statues have been shown to be perfectly ground and polished convex lenses...[T]he existence of these crystal eyes of such perfect workmanship proves that the technology for advanced optics [lens manufacture] existed in ancient Egypt.*"[2] But there is additional collaborating evidence:

- The Great Pyramid rests upon a cleared rock foundation which had been smoothed over a thirteen acre area with an incredible flatness, of +/- 0.001" per foot. Even the modern machine shop's Computer Numerical Control milling machines have trouble holding this type of tolerance over a single square-foot plate – let alone over a thirteen-acre surface. The ONLY known way to level a surface to this degree of flatness is with optical surveying equipment.

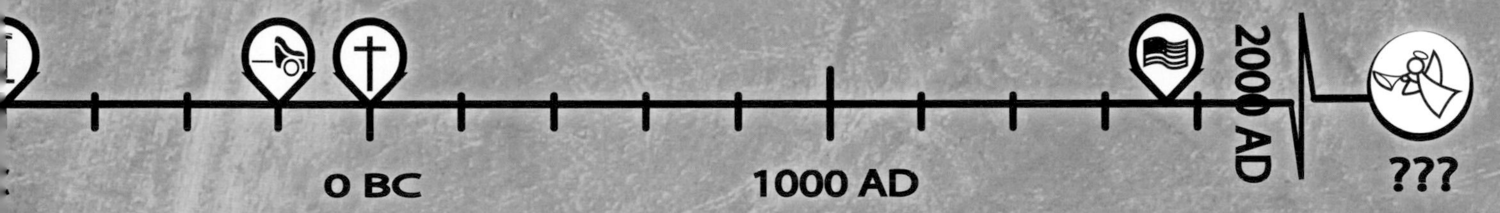

- The Rings of Saturn are invisible to the naked eye and can only be seen through a telescope. Yet the Ancient Egyptians describe Saturn as having rings.

- Sirius is a distant binary star system which appears as a single point of light unless viewed through a telescope. Yet the ancient Egyptians not only described Sirius as two stars, but accurately recorded the time period of the orbit of Sirius B around Sirius A. And it wasn't only the Egyptians who seemed to have possessed the knowledge of lenses. Shown on this page is an ancient burial stone from Peru portraying a man using a telescope to view what is apparently a comet. Also in Peru, the Nazca spider is a huge drawing etched into the desert floor (page 92). This famous artwork displays an accurate depiction of not just the rare Recinulei spider, but includes an organ at the end of one of its legs which is so small it can only be seen with the aid of a magnifying lens.

- Hair carving is an extremely ancient Chinese tradition. Those practicing this art form use lenses to aid them as they actually carve things upon a human hair. On the fragments of oracle bones of the Western Zhou period, unearthed in Guyuan, Shaanxi Province, there have been found small carved characters the size of rice grains with hair-thin strokes. Archeologists have also found 3400-year-old engravings on a millet grain, legible only under a five-fold magnification.[3] The fact that the Ancient Chinese were able to carve images only visible under a 5x magnification, is strong evidence that the use of magnifying lenses goes back more than 3000 years.

When it comes to the use of optical instruments to magnify objects either too small or too far away to be seen with the naked eye, the evidence is overwhelming that ancient people possessed the necessary technology. It is modern man, blinded by his preconceptions of "ignorant ancient humans," who seems to need assistance to see the obvious.

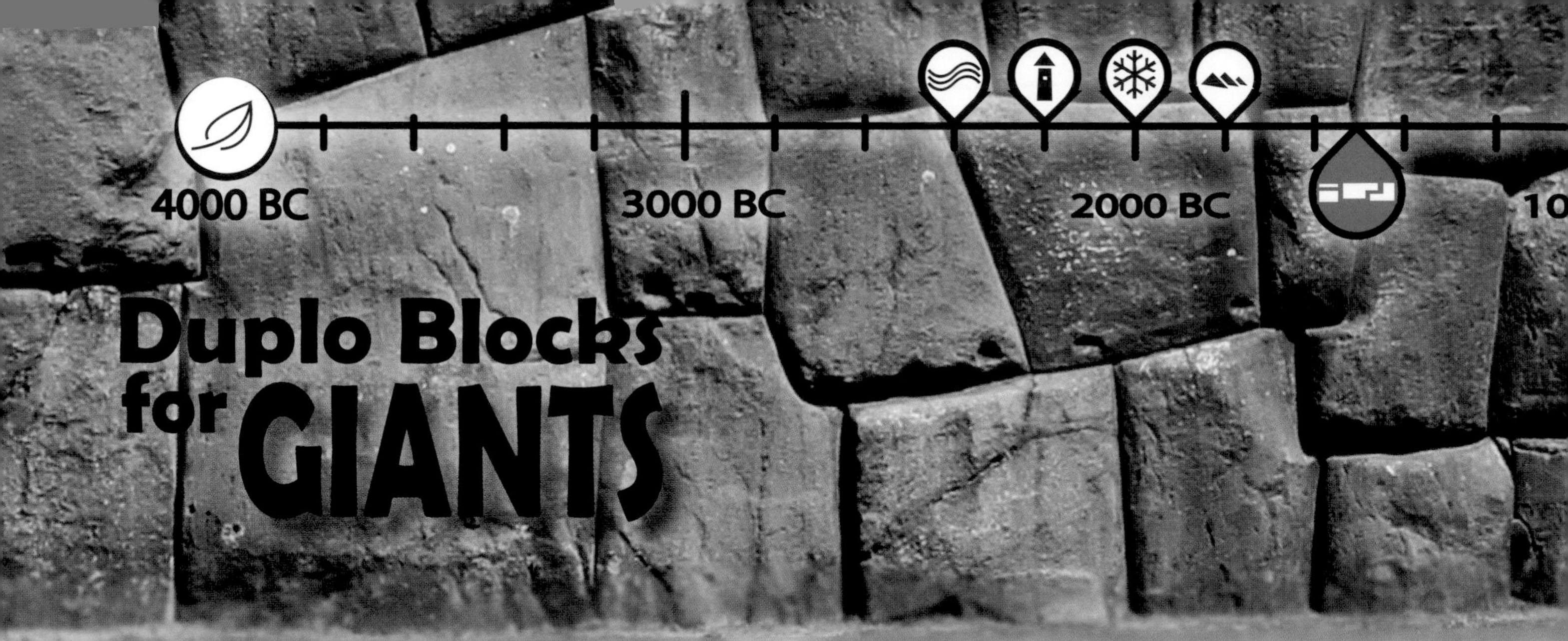

Duplo Blocks for GIANTS

Scientists like to use technical verbage. A "megalith" is a large stone which has been used to build a structure or monument, either alone or together with other stones. It requires advanced technology plus ingenuity to cut, move, and assemble such enormous stones. The origin of humanity is closely tied to the origin of technology. There are two basic explanations for the development of mankind's technology (and his physical body). By examining the capabilities of ancient civilizations, it becomes apparent which viewpoint of technology development is supported by the archeological evidence.

1. Mankind came from some lower (less intelligent) form of animal life and slowly increased in intelligence and ability. If this is the case, all forms of technology – language/communications, mathematics/astronomy, engineering/building - must have started out crude and increased in sophistication over time.

2. Mankind was created in God's image and therefore had extreme creativity and abilities from the very beginning. Knowledge and technology would have built upon developments made in previous generations, but highly advanced abilities would have been apparent from the very start.

Pictured on this page is an ancient Peruvian building site known as Saqsaywaman (pronounced 'sexy-woman' by locals). This enormous structure is typical of monstrous construction projects surviving from many ancient civilizations which developed around the world shortly after the flood of Noah. The enormous blocks of limestone (some weighing over 400,000 pounds) were cut to exact shapes to perfectly interlock like giant Duplo™ blocks, forming a lower wall capable of withstanding thousands of years of earthquakes and weathering.[1] Many researchers believe the lowest level of the wall (with the megalithic stones) was an original structure upon which the more recent Inca civilization added additions a few thousand years later.

There are still profound mysteries surrounding this 3000- to 4000-year-old structure:

- Why use such enormous blocks when the same type of structure could have been built more easily using smaller blocks?
- How were the 200-ton stones transported through mountainous terrain from quarries over twenty miles away?
- The stones are cut to perfectly nest one atop the next in intricate shapes. The fit is so exact that nowhere along the line of contact can you fully insert a credit card.

These "mysteries" are only mysterious because researchers are blinded by their starting assumption (the assumption that ancient man was less intelligent than modern man). By applying a Biblical framework to the ancient structure, its origin is easily explained. Immediately after the worldwide flood, humanity embarked upon a massive building project which may have required enormous stone blocks for its foundation (the Tower of Babel). Isn't it logical that people spreading out from here to locations around the world would mimic something familiar (megalithic structures made from enormous blocks of stone) at the new location in which they settled?

It is possible that a wetted bed of slick clay or multiple crisscrossed roller beds could have facilitated the movement of the massive blocks. However, that would have required extensive knowledge of civil engineering, mechanical engineering, material design, and extreme ingenuity and intelligence - exactly what the Biblical model of early mankind would predict.

The intricate shapes of these mammoth blocks is also a mystery for modern researchers because they assume ancient mankind did not have knowledge of modern technology such as wire, vibration, or rotational cutting techniques. It is typically taught that rubbing a hard abrasive "grit" over a stone surface or the use of chisels or water-soaked expanding wedges was used to create the flat, matching profiles.[1] Yet when tested, all of these techniques fail to produce perfectly flat profiles between blocks (see the next page). Ancient man clearly had the capability to work with metals (Genesis 4:22) and apparently had much more advanced cutting techniques than commonly assumed. It is only a philosophical blindness which requires a dumbed-down, early humanity that makes the cutting of these stones a process requiring lengthy rubbing with grit or slowly chipping away at the surfaces.

This archeological site is just one of a growing number of ancient discoveries showing the superiority of the Biblical model for mankind's origin, compared to the misleading assumptions of evolution – which require a belief in a brutish, ignorant early mankind.

PERU

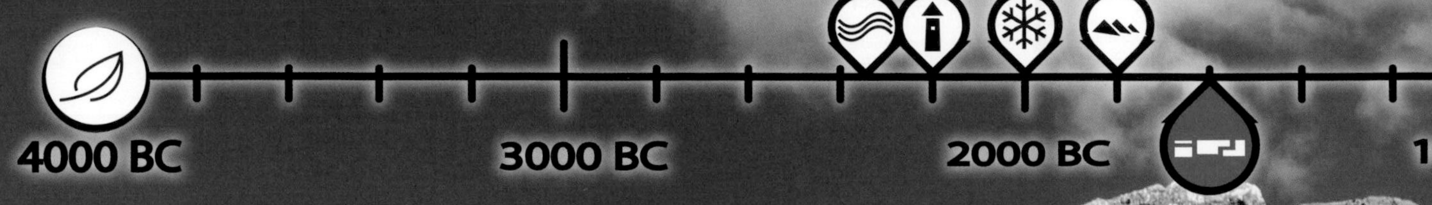

Foundations of Civilization

"I think he doth protest a bit too much." This classic cliché, about the lying perpetrator from many a murder-mystery novel, applies equally well to the defenders of the evolution-requiring time frame for everything. Belief in evolution mandates that advanced human technology must be relatively recent (in order to promote the idea that ancient man was more closely related to unintelligent ape-like creatures). A classic example is promoted in almost every book on the history of Peru - that the enormous structure at Saqsaywaman was built by the Incan empire within the last 1000 years. This is repeated so often, in so many places, that it is commonly accepted as fact by archeologists, tour guides, and the public at large who visit this ancient site. Yet glaring inconsistencies with this time frame are ignored.

Saqsaywaman was supposedly completed around 1508. It is believed to have taken 20,000 to 30,000 men over sixty years to complete the enormous structure. Most of the original structure was destroyed and used by the Spanish to build their homes after they conquered the Inca civilization. Yet Garcilaso de la Vega, a famed chronicler of the time, who was born in 1539 and raised in this area, seems not to have had a clue as to how this momentous structure was constructed. In describing Saqsaywaman (which had supposedly been completed less than twenty years before his birth, according to modern evolutionary-blinded archeologists) de la Vega wrote,

"It is indeed beyond the power of imagination to understand how these Indians, unacquainted with devices, engines, and implements, could have cut, dressed, raised, and lowered great rocks (more like lumps of hills than building stones), and set them so exactly in their positions. For this reason…the work is attributed to enchantment."

One would think a few of the 30,000 laborers doing a construction project within fifty years of someone recording the event would still be around and thus, the construction would not be attributed to "construction by enchantment." This testifies to the reality that the lower structure is much, much older than commonly taught. The Inca no doubt learned from and added to the structure, and it was these later (and smaller) stones which were removed by the Spanish to build their homes. But the original foundation stones were too large to move, even by the more "civilized and advanced" European invaders, and they remain in position to this day. They were likely laid down by a far more ancient and advanced culture which inhabited the area shortly after the dispersion from the Tower of Babel.

A wide variety of proposals have been suggested for how the stones were cut and shaped. Yet none of the current explanations fit the facts. Archaeologists Bingham (1913), Frank (1980), and Protzen (1986) proposed shaping stones using quartzite hammers. But on a microscopic level there are no signs of the proposed quartzite hammering of these granite (thirty percent quartz content) stone building blocks with a Mohs hardness of seven. Furthermore, inside corners could be no smaller than the radius of the hammers or chisels used, yet some of the corners of the fitted blocks have a radius in the thousandths of an inch range - such that an almost air-tight seal is produced, even at the corners of each stone. Modern stone fitters cannot achieve such precision. Rock also tends to break unevenly at the chiseled surface, and these rocks show no sign of this. For all of these reasons, the shaping by hammers and chisels simply cannot explain their appearance.

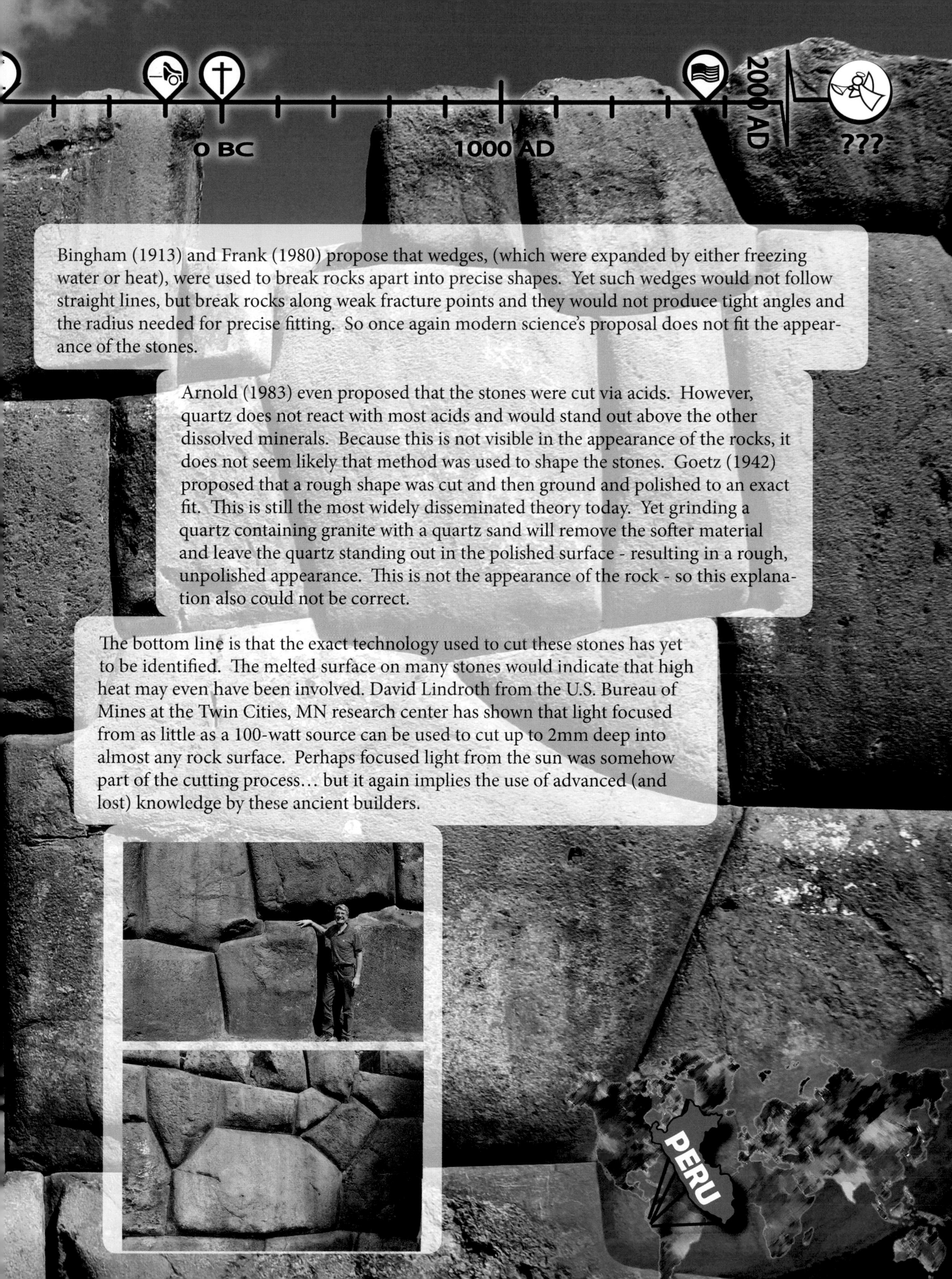

Bingham (1913) and Frank (1980) propose that wedges, (which were expanded by either freezing water or heat), were used to break rocks apart into precise shapes. Yet such wedges would not follow straight lines, but break rocks along weak fracture points and they would not produce tight angles and the radius needed for precise fitting. So once again modern science's proposal does not fit the appearance of the stones.

Arnold (1983) even proposed that the stones were cut via acids. However, quartz does not react with most acids and would stand out above the other dissolved minerals. Because this is not visible in the appearance of the rocks, it does not seem likely that method was used to shape the stones. Goetz (1942) proposed that a rough shape was cut and then ground and polished to an exact fit. This is still the most widely disseminated theory today. Yet grinding a quartz containing granite with a quartz sand will remove the softer material and leave the quartz standing out in the polished surface - resulting in a rough, unpolished appearance. This is not the appearance of the rock - so this explanation also could not be correct.

The bottom line is that the exact technology used to cut these stones has yet to be identified. The melted surface on many stones would indicate that high heat may even have been involved. David Lindroth from the U.S. Bureau of Mines at the Twin Cities, MN research center has shown that light focused from as little as a 100-watt source can be used to cut up to 2mm deep into almost any rock surface. Perhaps focused light from the sun was somehow part of the cutting process… but it again implies the use of advanced (and lost) knowledge by these ancient builders.

Massive Mining Operations

Most people have heard of the "Bronze Age," but few comprehend the amazing scope of this period of human history. The widespread use of bronze likely preceded the widespread use of iron because it melts at a lower temperature and is generally easier to work with. As long as an adequate supply of this metal was available, there was little incentive to produce weapons, statues, artwork, and implements from other metals. Thus, bronze (an alloy of copper with tin) and brass (an alloy of copper with zinc) has been widely used from 3800 years ago to the present. But few people have stopped to ponder from where the major component for bronze (i.e. copper) came.

Based on the number of bronze artifacts found from ancient cultures throughout Europe, Africa, South America, the Far East, and the Middle East, it has been conservatively estimated that over a 2000-year period, from 2000 BC to 0 BC, over one BILLION pounds of copper was used to make bronze artifacts.[1] Yet no significant copper mining seems to have occurred anywhere throughout Europe, the Middle East, or Africa until 1000 AD, and for the next 350 years a minuscule 2,000 tons was produced. So from where did all the copper needed to supply the bronze appetite for the ancient world come?

The world's richest location for pure copper ore is in the Upper Peninsula of Michigan (the three-pound pure copper nugget shown to the right was found in Keweenaw Peninsula, and is similar to what would have been mined in ancient times). From 1840 until 1890 more money was made from copper mining in Michigan than from all the gold mining of either the California or the Alaskan gold rushes of the 1800s. For instance, in 1869, ninety-five percent of all copper mined in the U.S. came from the Upper Peninsula of Michigan. Yet there is extensive evidence that the area was mined for copper more than 3000 years earlier.[2] To date, over 5000 ancient mines have been identified in just one area of upper Michigan, covering a seam of copper-rich ore 140 miles long by seven miles wide. In addition, Isle Royale is located off the Michigan mainland and has numerous mines located in an area five miles wide and forty miles long. These mining operations average thirty feet deep and twenty-five feet wide and, if placed end to end, would create a trench five miles long.[3]

Ancient copper mining techniques used in the British Isles consisted of building huge fires on veins of copper ore and then pouring water on top of the heated stone. This cracked the rock and allowed removal of the copper from the rock matrix. Not coincidentally, both the early Brits and the Phoenicians were accomplished sailors[4] and show evidence of extensive trade with the Middle East prior to 3000 years ago. The size of the Michigan mines indicate that up to 10,000 tons of ore was removed from each hole, yielding approximately fifty tons of pure copper. This would easily account for the billion pounds of copper used throughout the Bronze Age. If this ore was not shipped to Europe during this period of human history, what happened to all the mined copper? Not even one percent of the total copper removed from these 3000-year-old mines has been found in North American artifacts.

The massive scale of these mining operations, the efficiency with which the copper was shipped back to Europe, and the secrecy with which the trading nations apparently cloaked the source of their wealth all testify to the advanced ability and intelligence of early mankind.

0 BC
1000 AD
2000 AD
???
U.S.A.

THE ORIGINAL CONEHEADS

An old Saturday Night Live comedy routine involved people with long pointy heads who were called "cone-heads." This may have been inspired by the discovery of ancient skulls from Peru where people literally had cone-shaped skulls. From where did these strange skulls come? Why did these people wish to have octopus-shaped heads? How did they shape their skulls this way?

Babies are born with multiple soft, bony, unfused plates within their skulls. This is important for several reasons. First, it allows the baby's head to deform into an elongated shape as the baby is squeezed through its mother's birth canal during the birth of the infant. Second, it allows the skull to easily expand as the brain of the child rapidly grows during the first few years of his life when his brain is growing at a more rapid rate than at any other time in his life. However, the fact that the skull is soft and malleable during early childhood development also allows for its manipulation. The ancient Incas must have understood and utilized this fact.

It is not known why the ancient Peruvians deformed their skulls, but the practice seemed to have been limited to the royal upper classes. The oldest examples of skull deformation go back to the very beginning of Peru's history – almost 4000 years ago.[1] Speculation surrounding the reasons for the practice range from the desire to differentiate the royal class to the desire to influence brain function. Regardless of the reason, the ability to do this displays a remarkable understanding of human anatomy.

Skull manipulation was accomplished using techniques involving great patience, planning, and pain. Immediately after babies were born, boards were strapped to each side of a child's head, and a rope was used to tightly compress the boards together. It would be quite similar to walking around with a vice attached to your skull and each day having the vice squeezed a little tighter. This process would have continued during the entire time the child was growing - right up through his teenage years. The result was a brain and skull which grew in the only unrestrained direction - up and away from the face - producing a cone-shaped head and no forehead. Imagine the years of pain, constant pressure, and headaches these children must have had to endure as their skulls were being compressed and misshapen. Interestingly, this is not the only culture where this practice shows up - the second wife of Egyptian Pharoah Rameses II (Nefertiti) also had such a shaped skull.

Throughout human history, people have used inventive (and often painful) ways to modify their body appearance. One tribe in Africa places rings around a woman's neck in order to force her collarbones downward - giving her a long giraffe-like neck appearance. Other cultures put increasingly larger discs into holes in their earlobes until they are stretched almost down to their shoulders. The Chinese have been known to grow fingernails so long that they reach to the floor…while other cultures cover their entire bodies with tattoos. Beauty really is in the eye of the beholder!

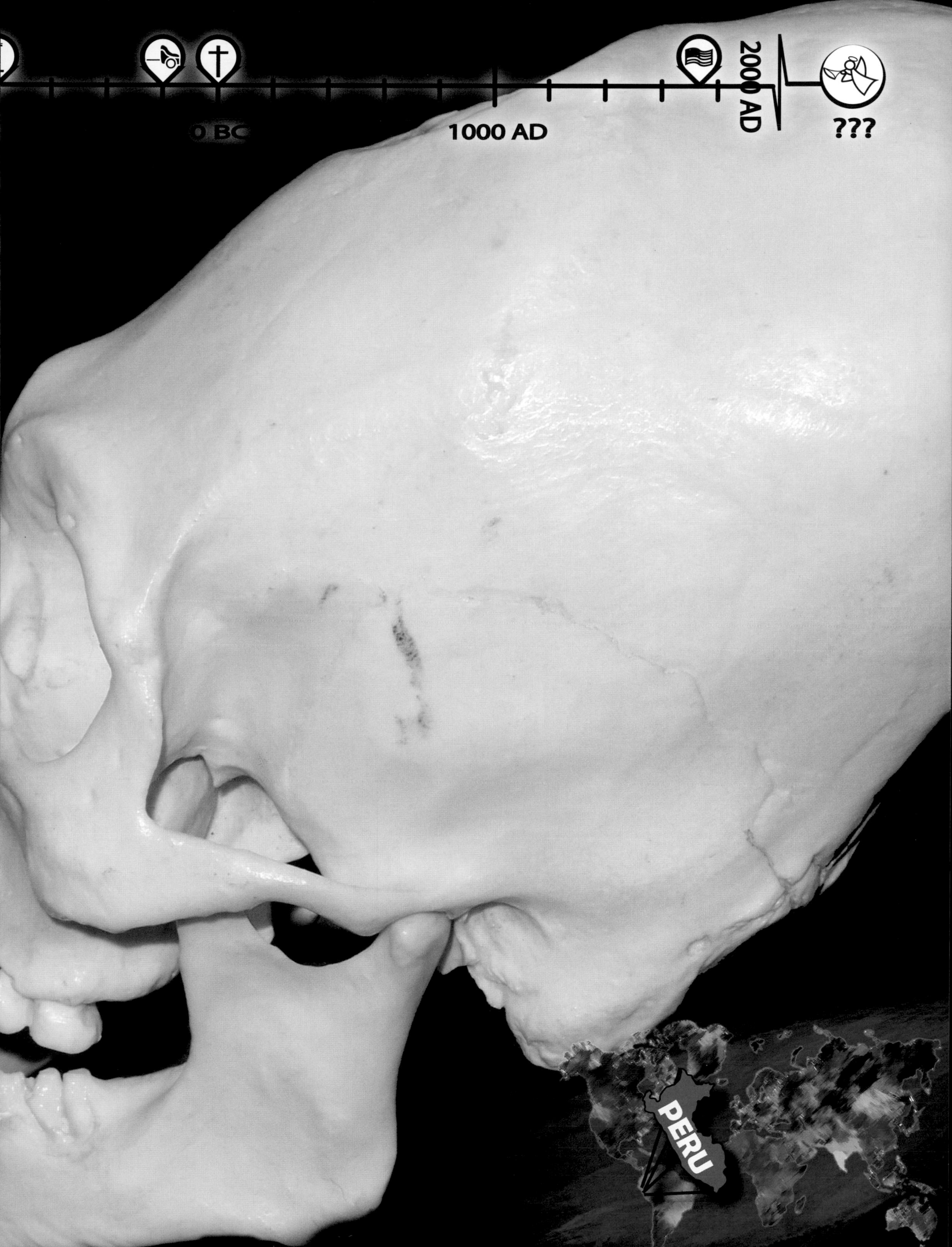

0 BC
1000 AD
2000 AD
???
PERU

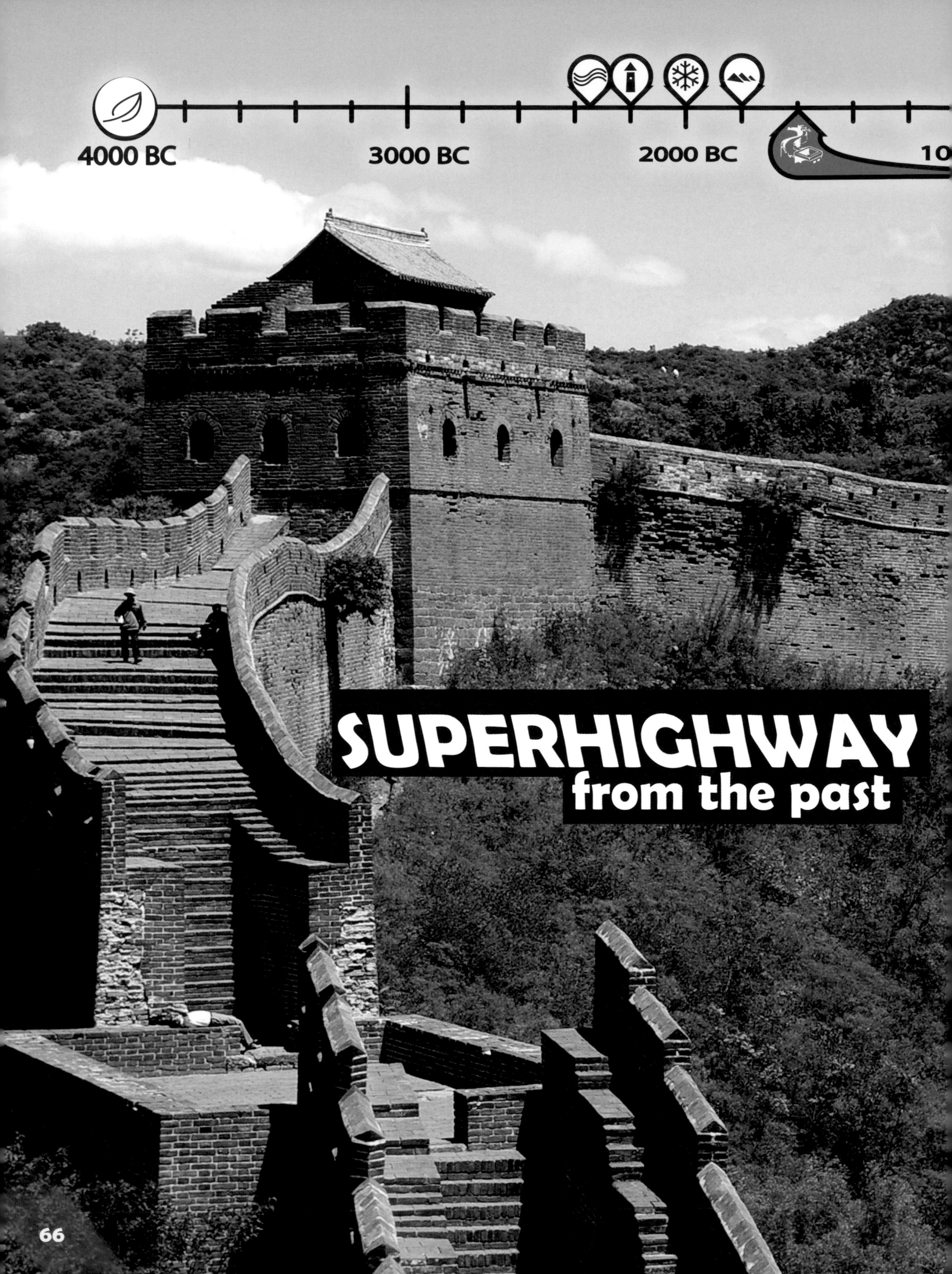

SUPERHIGHWAY from the past

The Great Wall of China, although neither as grandiose as the Egyptian pyramids, nor the only manmade object visible from space (desert roads actually are more visible), is still a marvel testifying to the brilliance, perseverance, and ingenuity of mankind. This archeological marvel has been called, *"One of the most stunning achievements of mankind"* and is on the list of the ten greatest wonders ever built by ancient mankind.[1] Originally started 3600 years ago by individual kingdoms as a way to defend their territories from other war lords, dozens of individual sections of the wall were rebuilt and combined to form the "Great Wall" under the leadership of Qin Shi Huangdi (see page 94) about 2200 years ago.[2]

The original wall construction technique was simple but innovative. A wood or bamboo framework was packed with dirt and hardened into a 6- to 8-inch thick layer. The mold was then moved up, and the next eight-inch layer was packed on top, until each section of the ten- to thirty-foot-tall wall was completed. Billions of pounds of earth had to be moved and packed into place to make these original wall sections. Qin Shi Huangdi took the modernization and extension of the project to new heights (and lengths).

During his reign, the older individual sections of the wall were rebuilt and extended using sun-baked bricks. Towers over forty feet tall were added at regular intervals and spaced such that archers could defend every square foot of the wall. A fifteen to twenty-five foot wide super highway was built across the top of its entire 13,170-mile length.[3] Even more significant than the defense which the wall offered, this highway allowed ease of travel and communication between the fifteen enormous provinces throughout unified China. Hundreds of thousands of workers were involved in this massive building project, which continued with major improvements up to the 14th century. Transportation was critical in ruling a country as large as China, and it is not insignificant that the Chinese are credited with the invention of horse-drawn chariots and wagons with uniform axle widths (making it easier to standardize road construction). Also in the area of transportation innovations, the Chinese invented the first truly movable rudder for ships (making them easier to steer) - hundreds of years before Western civilizations developed the same technology.[4]

The Great Wall was started within 1000 years of people settling in China from Babel, and construction and use of the wall continued for more than 3000 years. Many parts of the wall continue to exist to this day, another testimony to the ability and genius of ancient mankind.

LANDSCAPING on a massive scale

Anthropologists, steeped in evolutionary preconceptions, believe that North and South America were home to nothing more than small bands of roving natives for tens of thousands of years. It is commonly taught that this primitive and insignificant population of humans did little to impact the environment until quite recently. These anthropologists fail to see obvious contradictions to the blinding impact of their philosophic viewpoint, even when the truth is blatantly obvious. A perfect example can be seen in the Beni province of Bolivia.

This area of Bolivia, the size of Illinois and Indiana put together (and nearly as flat), is covered with water from the overflowing upper tributaries of the Amazon for half of the year and is essentially a desert for the rest of the year. In 1961 a doctoral geography student, William Denevan, came to Bolivia and noted that large swaths of the terrain throughout the Beni were crisscrossed with *"long, straight, raised berms, canals, raised agricultural fields, moat-like ditches, and zigzagging ridges."* According to Denevan and others who followed him, *"[T]hese things were not natural. You just don't have that kind of straight lines in nature."* To further the mystery, the area hosts hundreds of mounds (many up to sixty feet tall) which are filled with pieces of broken pottery shards and other signs of advanced human habitation. A similar mound outside of southeast Rome is called Monte Testaccio and served as the trash dump for the entire city of Rome for hundreds of years. Imagine the size and duration of the population needed to produce 100 such trash dumps, and you begin to understand the difficulty modern historians (who believe only a few people ever lived in this area) have in accepting that these mounds and ditches are the result of human civilization. The statement of Dr. Betty Meggers of the Smithsonian Institution is typical of the consensus thinking of modern archeologists who are blinded by their preconceptions: *"I have seen no evidence that large numbers of people ever lived in the Beni... [C]laiming otherwise is just wishful thinking."*[1] Yet consensus does not determine truth. So how do discoveries such as the Beni canals and mounds fit into a Biblical view of Earth history?

To transform thousands of square miles and produce enormous earthen mounds would require many years and the efforts of hundreds of thousands of people. There is every indication that this massive land-altering process was the result of burning entire forests and moving monumental amounts of dirt in order to produce fish weirs for food harvesting, to build extensive raised villages for habitation, to dig widespread canals for transportation/communication, and to construct countless moats/palisades for defense. It is possible that this area was inhabited for over 3000 years – only to be wiped out as the Spanish, in their all-consuming quest for gold, ravaged the entire continent only 500 years ago.

Essentially nothing is known about the civilization which altered the landscape of this entire region, but the industry, inventiveness, and impact on the landscape is apparent. Yet it is this very inventiveness and the amazing scope of ancient man's achievements which blind otherwise brilliant researchers to the acknowledgement that this area is, indeed, the result of early human civilization – apparently starting briefly after the dispersion of humanity from Babel.

0 BC
1000 AD
2000 AD
???
BOLIVIA

Texas-Sized Marbles

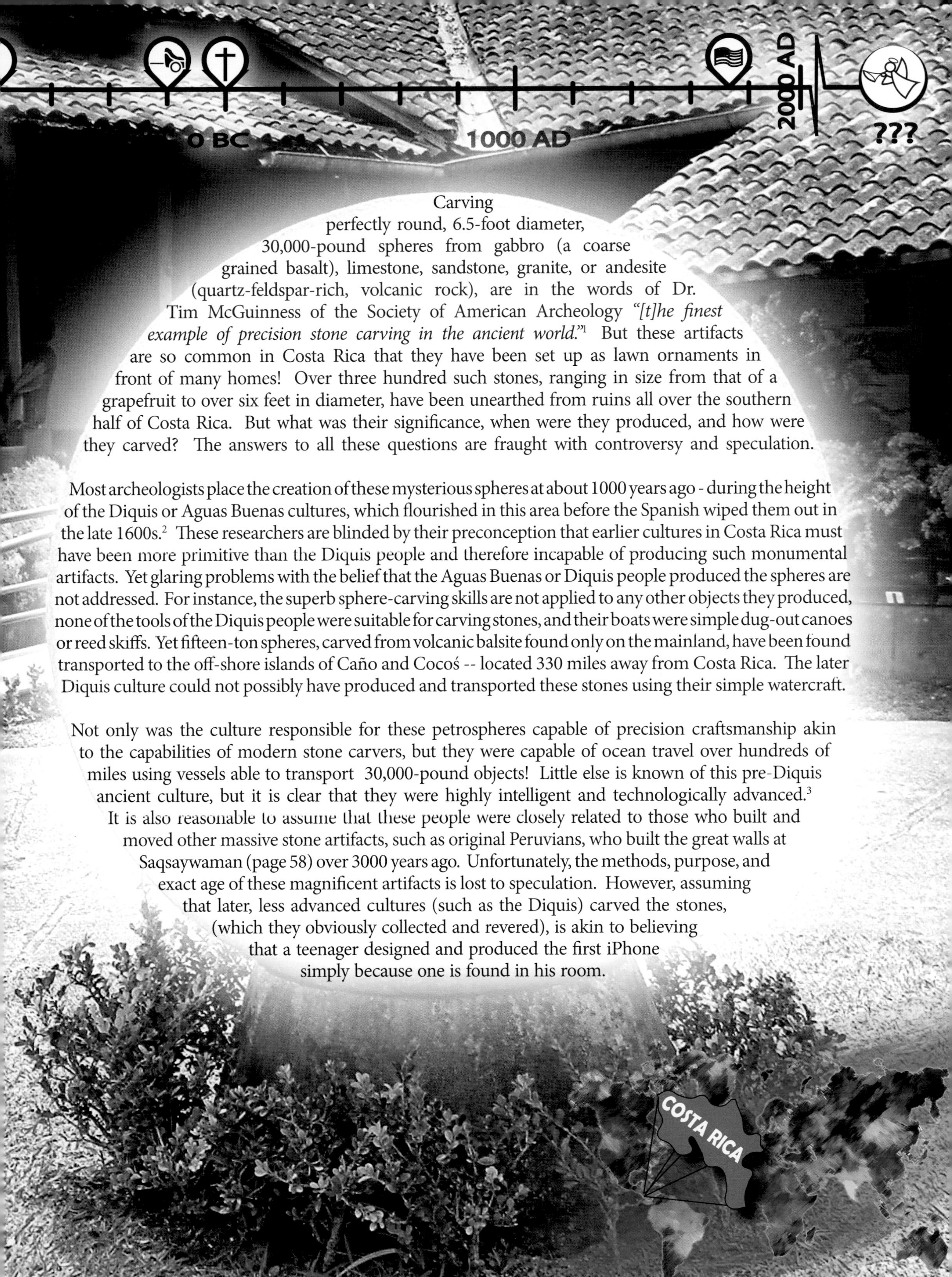

Carving perfectly round, 6.5-foot diameter, 30,000-pound spheres from gabbro (a coarse grained basalt), limestone, sandstone, granite, or andesite (quartz-feldspar-rich, volcanic rock), are in the words of Dr. Tim McGuinness of the Society of American Archeology *"[t]he finest example of precision stone carving in the ancient world."*[1] But these artifacts are so common in Costa Rica that they have been set up as lawn ornaments in front of many homes! Over three hundred such stones, ranging in size from that of a grapefruit to over six feet in diameter, have been unearthed from ruins all over the southern half of Costa Rica. But what was their significance, when were they produced, and how were they carved? The answers to all these questions are fraught with controversy and speculation.

Most archeologists place the creation of these mysterious spheres at about 1000 years ago - during the height of the Diquis or Aguas Buenas cultures, which flourished in this area before the Spanish wiped them out in the late 1600s.[2] These researchers are blinded by their preconception that earlier cultures in Costa Rica must have been more primitive than the Diquis people and therefore incapable of producing such monumental artifacts. Yet glaring problems with the belief that the Aguas Buenas or Diquis people produced the spheres are not addressed. For instance, the superb sphere-carving skills are not applied to any other objects they produced, none of the tools of the Diquis people were suitable for carving stones, and their boats were simple dug-out canoes or reed skiffs. Yet fifteen-ton spheres, carved from volcanic balsite found only on the mainland, have been found transported to the off-shore islands of Caño and Cocoś -- located 330 miles away from Costa Rica. The later Diquis culture could not possibly have produced and transported these stones using their simple watercraft.

Not only was the culture responsible for these petrospheres capable of precision craftsmanship akin to the capabilities of modern stone carvers, but they were capable of ocean travel over hundreds of miles using vessels able to transport 30,000-pound objects! Little else is known of this pre-Diquis ancient culture, but it is clear that they were highly intelligent and technologically advanced.[3] It is also reasonable to assume that these people were closely related to those who built and moved other massive stone artifacts, such as original Peruvians, who built the great walls at Saqsaywaman (page 58) over 3000 years ago. Unfortunately, the methods, purpose, and exact age of these magnificent artifacts is lost to speculation. However, assuming that later, less advanced cultures (such as the Diquis) carved the stones, (which they obviously collected and revered), is akin to believing that a teenager designed and produced the first iPhone simply because one is found in his room.

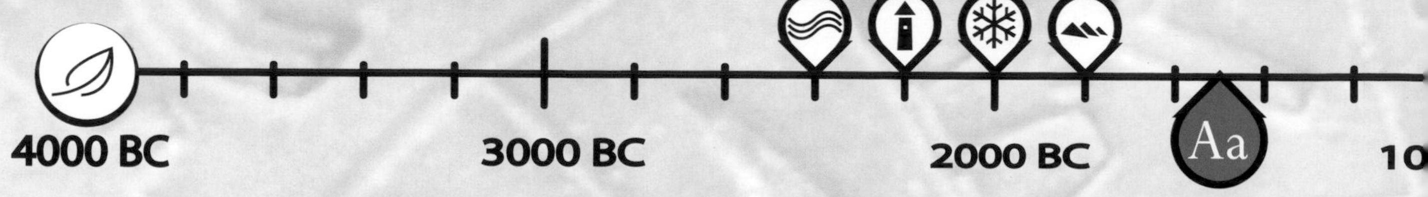

Ancient Movable Print

Historians point to one event as the major factor which moved mankind out of the Dark Ages and ushered in the Renaissance (1450 - 1650), the Reformation (1517 - 1700), the Enlightenment (1650 - 1800), and the Scientific Revolution (1550 - 1850). That event was the invention of the printing press. It was the discovery that movable type could be used to mass-produce writing (credited to Johannes Gutenberg in 1440) which changed the Western world and distinguished this inventor as the most influential human to live in the last 1000 years.[1] For thousands of years prior to this invention, the transfer of knowledge from one generation to the next was either via verbal tradition or the laborious practice of hand-copying documents. The slow advance of technology in this area may have been by design because knowledge is power, and an ignorant population is easier to control - as demonstrated by ruthless governments and dictators throughout history (who have opposed education for minorities, slaves, and women). Thus the incentive by rulers to create a widely educated populace, with easy access to printed materials, was not a priority.

It is also notable that the Bible was one of the first books to be printed and widely distributed on a printing press. There are only twenty-one known copies of the original Gutenberg Bible, and they are worth an estimated $20,000,000 each.[2] Amidst much controversy, the Bible was rapidly reproduced in German (and later English), in order that the "man-on-the-street" could understand and apply its truths to both his personal life and his government. It is a reasonable observation that the widespread distribution of God's Word was an underlying cause for the rapid advancement of human knowledge in both theology (the Reformation) and science (the Enlightenment) throughout the 1500 - 1800s.

But did mankind really first invent the printing press in Germany, or was this "rediscovered technology" which had been practiced thousands of years earlier but long forgotten? One of the most fascinating discoveries of ancient Greece is a clay disc discovered in 1908. Archeologist Luigi Pernier claimed to have found this amazing artifact in the main cell of an underground "temple depository" in the Minoan palace site of Phaistos (on the south coast of Crete, Greece). These basement cells, only accessible from above, were covered with a layer of fine plaster, filled with black earth, and mixed with the ashes of burnt cow bones. Amidst this mess was found a perfectly preserved clay disc buried about twenty inches above the floor level. This six-inch-diameter disc displays a series of 241 pictorial symbols spiraling toward the disc's center and arranged in "letter-like" fashion. The impressions on the clay

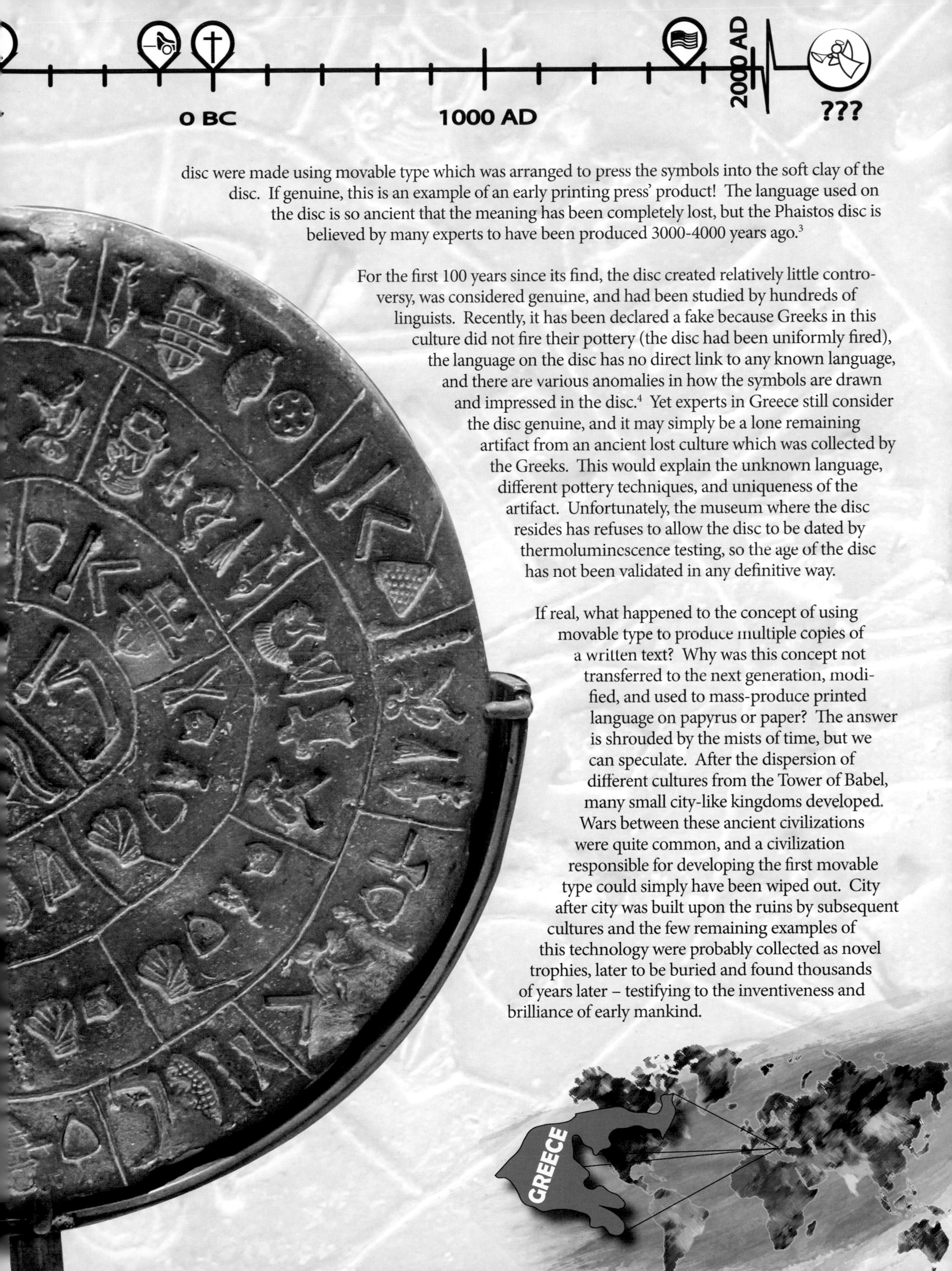

disc were made using movable type which was arranged to press the symbols into the soft clay of the disc. If genuine, this is an example of an early printing press' product! The language used on the disc is so ancient that the meaning has been completely lost, but the Phaistos disc is believed by many experts to have been produced 3000-4000 years ago.[3]

For the first 100 years since its find, the disc created relatively little controversy, was considered genuine, and had been studied by hundreds of linguists. Recently, it has been declared a fake because Greeks in this culture did not fire their pottery (the disc had been uniformly fired), the language on the disc has no direct link to any known language, and there are various anomalies in how the symbols are drawn and impressed in the disc.[4] Yet experts in Greece still consider the disc genuine, and it may simply be a lone remaining artifact from an ancient lost culture which was collected by the Greeks. This would explain the unknown language, different pottery techniques, and uniqueness of the artifact. Unfortunately, the museum where the disc resides has refuses to allow the disc to be dated by thermoluminescence testing, so the age of the disc has not been validated in any definitive way.

If real, what happened to the concept of using movable type to produce multiple copies of a written text? Why was this concept not transferred to the next generation, modified, and used to mass-produce printed language on papyrus or paper? The answer is shrouded by the mists of time, but we can speculate. After the dispersion of different cultures from the Tower of Babel, many small city-like kingdoms developed. Wars between these ancient civilizations were quite common, and a civilization responsible for developing the first movable type could simply have been wiped out. City after city was built upon the ruins by subsequent cultures and the few remaining examples of this technology were probably collected as novel trophies, later to be buried and found thousands of years later – testifying to the inventiveness and brilliance of early mankind.

The *REAL* Native Americans

Who doesn't remember the childhood rhyme commemorating the "discovery" of America: *"In 1492, Columbus sailed the ocean blue"*? Yet one of the great ignored anomalies of American history is the presence of ancient writings at dozens of locations across the United States which predate Columbus by thousands of years. These writings have been found on rock faces, boulders, tablets, and even metal plates at locations in New England, Michigan, Ohio, and all along the Mississippi River Valley.[1] The idea that people from various postflood cultures visited North America over 3000 years ago completely destroys the evolutionary idea that mankind had not developed commerce and civilization to a level allowing world travel during what they would have coined the "Stone Age" of Earth history. These writings have been ignored for many years and even attributed to plow scrapings or random doodling because they are from ancient alphabets of the Celts, Phoenicians, and Paleo-Hebrews (pre-Hebrew written language). Thus, in spite of hundreds of documented examples from dozens of locations, these ancient writings are simply ignored and not discussed in modern textbooks, as students are guided toward believing only the evolutionary view of world history. Yet there is a logical explanation for these ancient writings, which perfectly fits into the Biblical account of the Earth's history.

After the flood, highly intelligent people were capable of re-establishing travel, commerce, and navigational skills from the pre-flood world. These people were anxious to explore the newly restructured Earth, which had been *"deluged and destroyed"* (2 Peter 3:6), such that any post-flood sources of raw materials could be relocated. They were already skilled in building and metalworking, and would need new sources of raw materials/metals with which to rebuild civilization. As previously noted (see page 38), within 400 years of

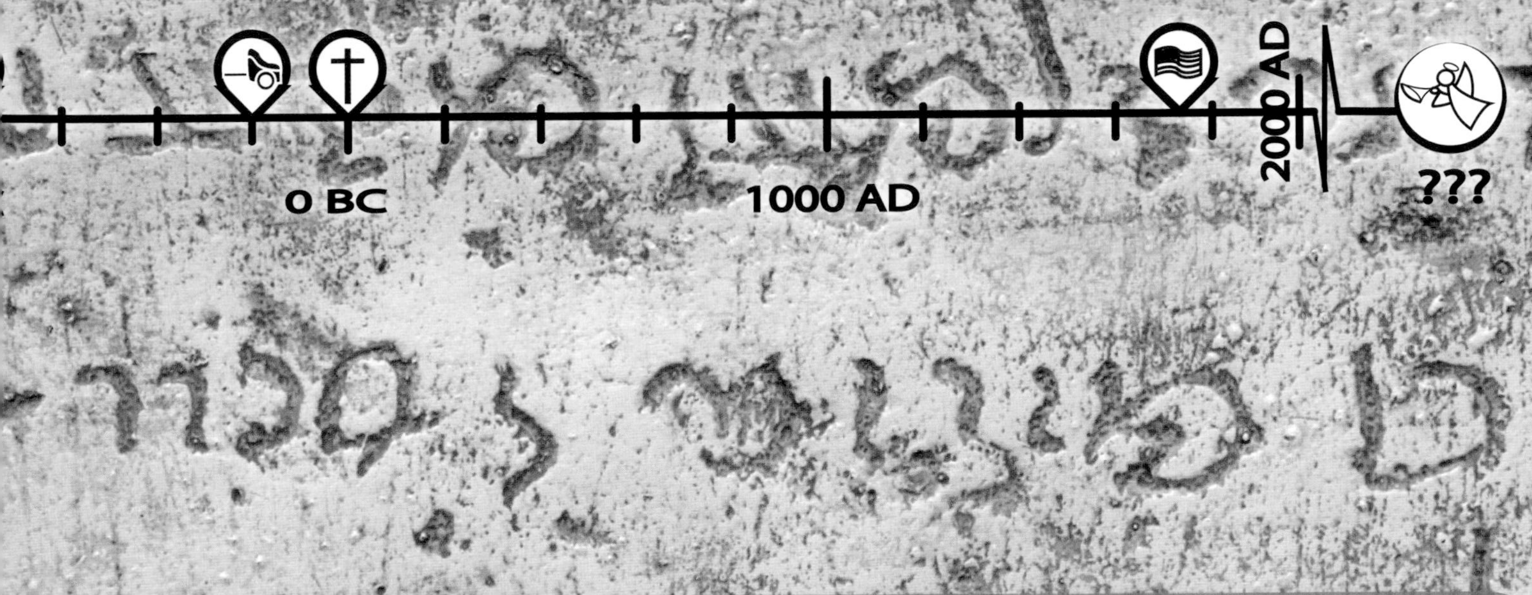

the flood, there could have been millions of people in many different cultural groups – plenty of people capable of sending out exploration parties around the world. Thus, finding evidence of writing from ancient people in North America should not be at all surprising. Even thirty years ago a brilliant Harvard linguist, Dr. Barry Fell, had documented beyond any reasonable doubt the existence of stone shrines, monuments, tablets, and cave shelters across New England, which contained inscriptions identical to ancient Celtic and Phoenician writings.[1] His extensive discoveries have largely been ignored because they do not fit into the "ignorant ancient man" timeline of academia. Both Celts and Phoenicians were known to have developed extensive sea travel which far exceeded Roman capabilities before the time of Roman sea domination (2200 years ago).[2] It would not be at all surprising that these people would have made extensive explorations into America a thousand years earlier than this – leaving behind shelters, shrines, and monuments. Ravaged by the passage of time, the unknown writing style was ignored by later European settlers and assumed to be of American Indian origin. Meanwhile, the MUCH earlier shelters and shrines from these 3000-year-old travelers were deconstructed for use in walls and new buildings.

So what happened to these developing outposts from 3000-year-old Middle Eastern and European civilizations? Either they died out, returned to Europe, or were assimilated into other branches of North Americans who migrated from the Pacific Northwest, and ultimately became what we know as the native North American Indian tribes. Over time the ties with their original roots became lost, just as most modern Americans, in spite of enormously advanced travel and communication abilities, have little contact or knowledge of their European or African ancestry. The unstable and often warring cultures of the Mediterranean area simply collapsed and cut off further exploration before the rise of the classic Greek civilization, isolating these early travelers in America.

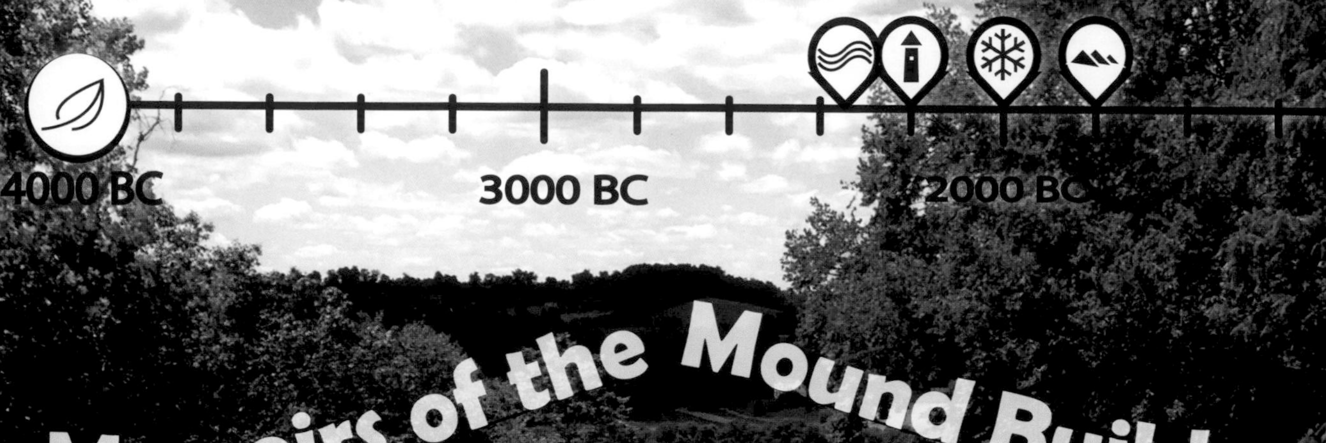

Memoirs of the Mound Builders

One of the greatest unsolved mysteries from America's Midwest is the origin of hundreds of mounds and earthworks which can be found throughout Ohio, Michigan, Kentucky, Indiana, and Pennsylvania. These earthworks range from mounds of earth up to seventy feet tall and three hundred feet in diameter - to intricately shaped snakes, complete with a head and coiled tail over 1300 feet in length - to intricate concentric geometric circles. There are almost as many theories as to their origin as there are web sites devoted to their existence.

Carbon-dated objects found within the mounds place their age at anywhere from 600 years to 3000 years. Radiocarbon dating back to 3000 years ago is relatively accurate so the mounds were likely built this early in Earth history. Carbon dating within 1000 years of the Flood is increasingly inaccurate because the Earth's atmosphere and biosphere were rapidly changing as a new equilibrium developed (from the steep change in atmospheric carbon levels caused by the Flood). It is likely that the 3000-year-old artifacts found within the mounds are from original builders, whereas the younger artifacts were simply added later by subsequent Native American cultures. The most common opinion is that these mounds were built by a race of extinct Native American settlers known as the Adena culture.[1] Little is known about their culture because they are believed to have flourished in this area of the country from 2000 to 3000 years ago, and left little evidence for their existence except for these extensive and massive mounds. The number and size of these earthen structures provides an understanding of their ability to organize massive building projects.

Especially intriguing are a series of slate, copper, and clay plates which were found in these mounds by amateur archeologists in Lower Michigan from 1850 - 1910.[2] A number of these plates were collected, photographed, and cataloged (along with their discovery location) in a book published in 1910.[3] Even though multiple eyewitnesses testified that they saw the plates being removed from undisturbed mounds and similar plates were found within widely separated mounds by different investigators throughout Michigan, these engravings have long been declared fakes and forgeries by the mainstream archeological community.[4] They are dismissed not because of any evidence surrounding their discovery, but primarily because of the images found upon the plates.

Shown on this page is just one of over forty ancient Adena engravings.[5] It is obvious that people of the Adena culture were flourishing in America over 3000 years ago because they had time to produce intricate engraving and build massive earthworks. They also possessed an intimate knowledge of the Flood of Noah and other Biblical events. Notice that on the third panel there is even a dove with an olive branch. The fourth panel shows animals coming off a huge boat in pairs while a man and three sons raise their hands in praise. With images such as these found on these engravings, it is little wonder that archeologists trained to believe that ancient man was an unsophisticated savage would reject them as fake. Yet they make perfect sense if these ancient people were, in reality, direct and recent descendants from Noah himself. These early settlers likely traveled to America after they separated from other people groups at the Tower of Babel. They obviously retained knowledge of the Flood and other historical events documented in the Bible.

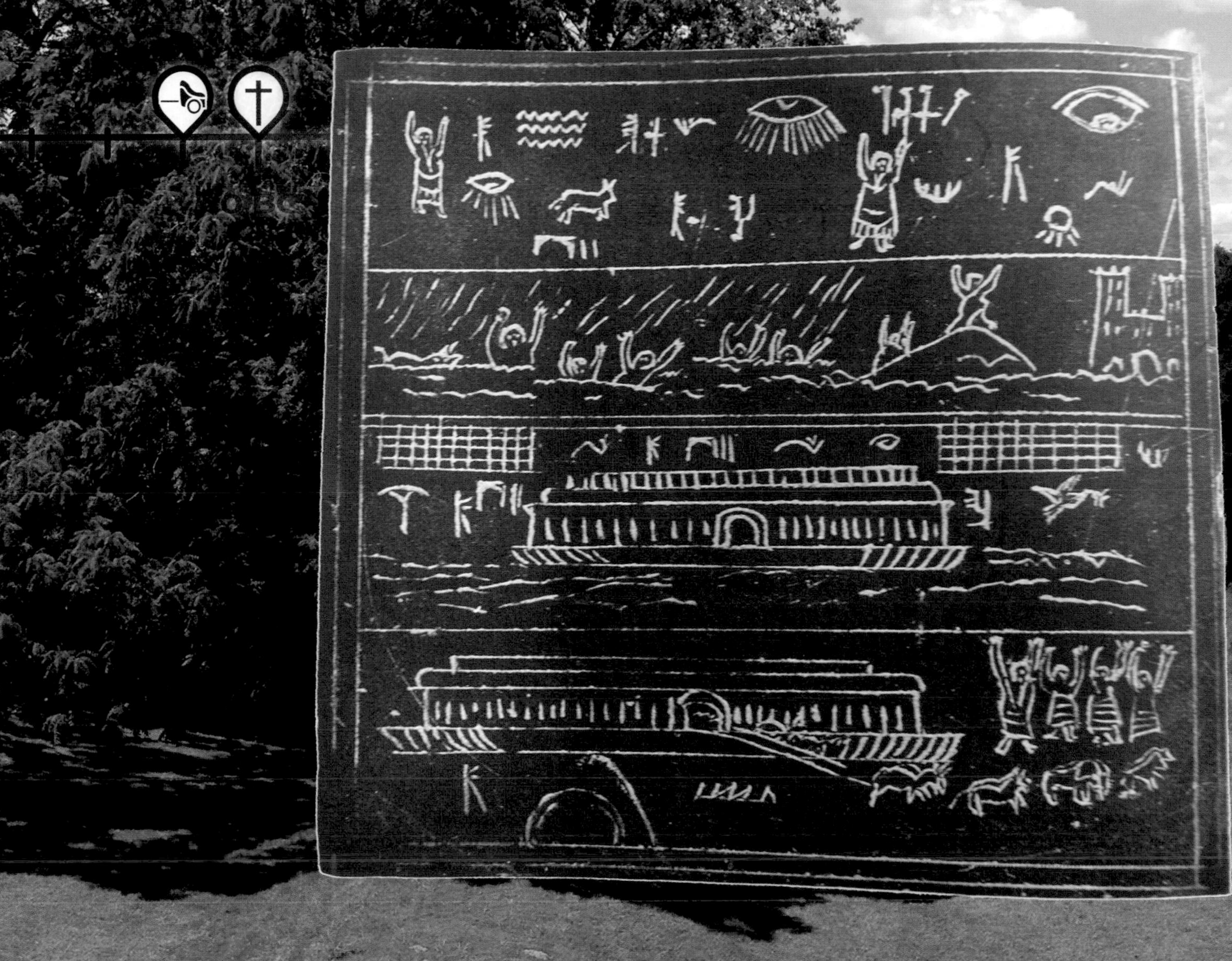

U.S.A.

TECHNOLOGY ADVANCEMENT
3000 TO 2000 YEARS AGO

This period of Earth history, more than any time until the last 200 years, is characterized by the incredibly rapid advancement of mankind's knowledge. By this time carbon-14 levels had begun to stabilize, so the actual age of most artifacts, especially later in this period, becomes more accurately measurable. Furthermore, the documentation of technology via written records, surviving structures, and pottery is far more commonplace -- allowing a more accurate picture of the capabilities of this period. It is the speed with which technologies and vast civilizations developed which testifies to the God-given creativity and inventiveness of mankind.

Previous to this period, two great civilizations seemed to dominate the Earth – the Egyptians and the Chinese. However, the Egyptian culture collapsed economically and socially in the middle of the second millennium BC (3500 years ago) as it was hit with a disastrous series of plagues, its military was destroyed, and its slave population left the country, taking with it most of the material wealth (the Exodus of the Israelites). China continued

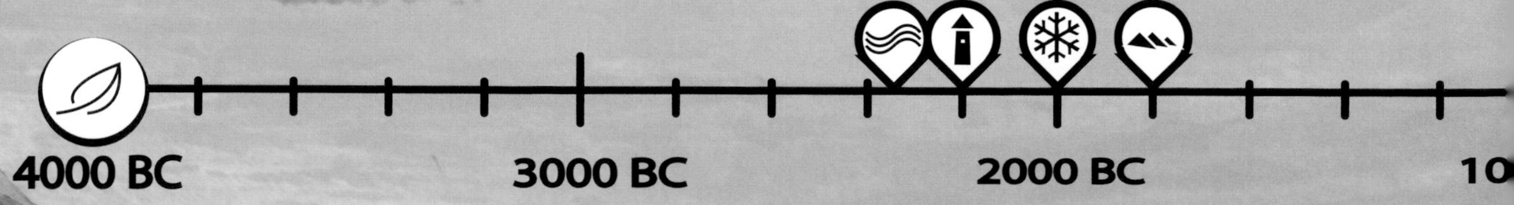

as a major culture, but failed to develop past its initial burst of technological advancement due to continual fighting between territorial lords. There is an even more important factor responsible for the stagnation of technological advancement in China. Originally, China worshiped and acknowledged one creator God (Shang-Ti), who had made everything. Therefore, the laws by which the universe operated could be discovered and understood. Later this was replaced by belief in Buddhism, whereby an infinitely old universe essentially made itself. This philosophic belief prevented anything from ever being known for sure and stagnated scientific progress.

During this period the rise of many extremely inventive world cultures exploded: the Greeks with their advancements in philosophy, art, architecture, mathematics, and theater; the Mayans/Aztecs/Incas with their developments in architecture, astronomy, and mathematics; massive cities in India with heated bathhouses and city-wide drainage systems; culminating with the Romans and their military expertise - enabling them to completely dominate Europe, the Middle East, and Northern Africa for centuries.
It was at the end of this period of time -- when mankind had the capability of understanding and rapidly spreading the truth about God's love around the world - that the greatest event since the creation of the universe occurred. The Maker of the universe entered into creation as a human being (Jesus Christ), in order to take the penalty for mankind's rebellion (death) upon Himself - so that mankind could return to fellowship with his Creator. For the first time since Adam and Eve, sinful mankind no longer had to continue in the struggle to earn his way back into the perfection of God's presence - a hopeless and futile effort which never works because we never know if we have been "good enough" or "done enough." In sacrificing Himself, God made it clear that it is only through faith in what He did for us that we can be saved. And that event transformed all of human history - leading directly to the final stage of human technological advancement.

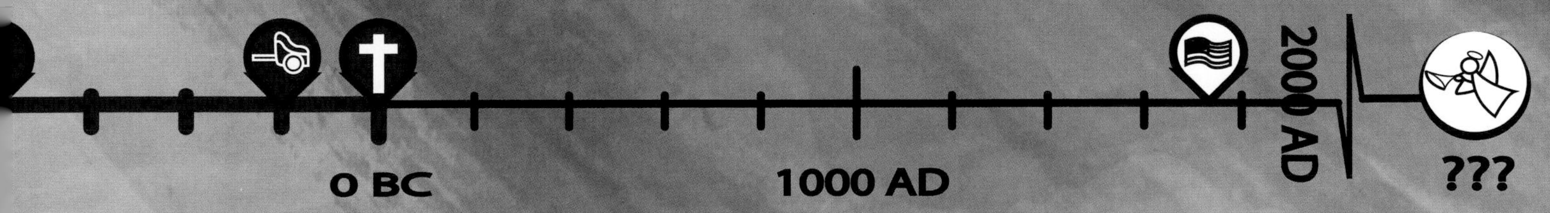

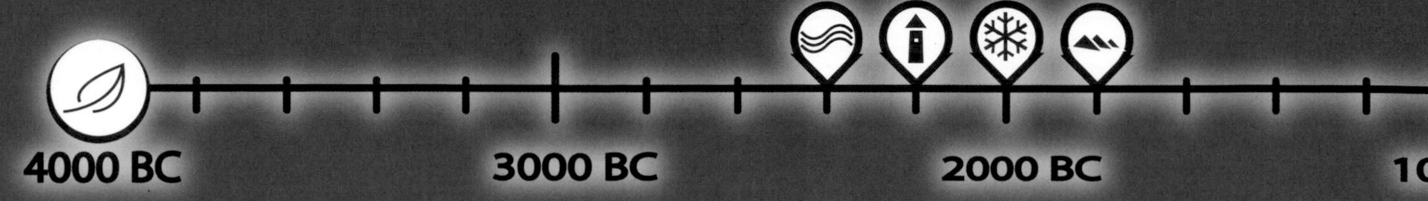

Mankind's Memory in Marble

The ancient Greek culture is revered for its advancements in philosophy, architecture, mathematics, and many other achievements. They are also remembered for their fanciful stories of multiple gods, which can be found everywhere throughout their society – in literature and on statues, pottery, monuments, and buildings. Every public school child is required to learn about the revered gods of the ancient Greeks. But where did they get the ideas for their "gods"? To answer this question, one must first understand the philosophy of these ancient people. To the Greeks, humanity was the pinnacle of creation and all things revolved around mankind and his abilities. This is why all of their gods took the form of humans, with all of humanity's problems, jealousies, and frailties. In their worldview, there is no Creator God, only ancestors, and submission to a Creator God was considered weakness, whereas independence from such an oppressive rule-maker was considered the height of virtue.

The second key to understanding the art and sculptures of the ancient Greeks - almost all of which were obsessed with their deities - is that these Greeks had a clear understanding of the same events of early humanity as are recorded in the Bible. Their culture was flourishing within a thousand years of the death of Noah, and their art makes it very apparent that they were familiar with the account of Adam and Eve, the entrance of sin and death into creation, the murder of Adam's son Abel by the hand of his brother Cain, the flood of Noah, and the rise of new cultures after Noah. They especially deify Eve (as she accepts what the serpent has to offer), Cain (as he escapes the repressive rules of his family), Noah's son Ham (who longs to possess the mantle of authority from his father Noah), and Noah's great grandson Nimrod (who ushers in a new order of man-centered religion). Noah is always portrayed in Greek sculptures and art as a timid old man associated with the sea whose power, children, and mantle of authority are being removed from him. All of the people recorded in the first eleven chapters of the Bible are prominently portrayed among the "gods" of ancient Greek mythology, but in Greek

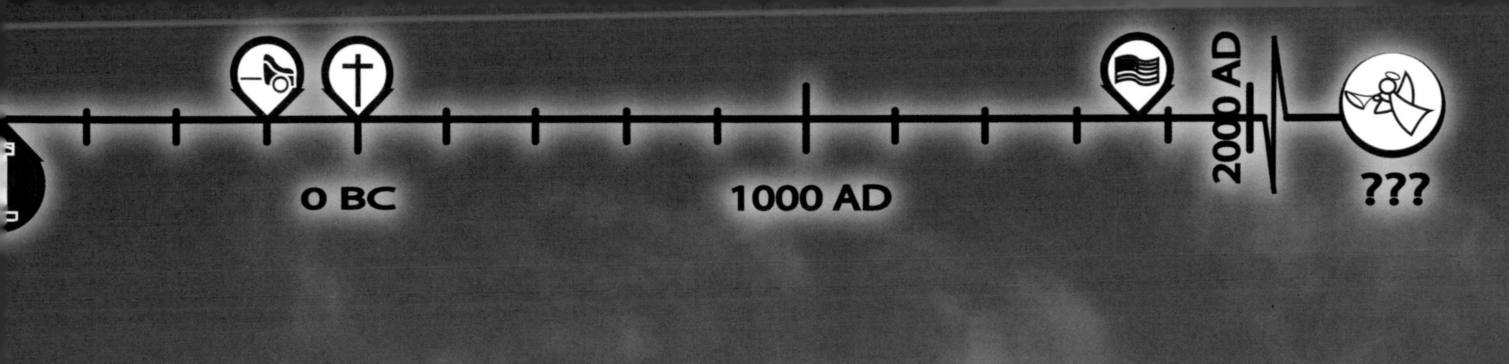

nythology these Biblical figures have been given different names and roles. Those who honor and obey a Creator God are ortrayed as powerless, while those in rebellion against the God of the Bible are portrayed as gods to be worshipped – the exact pposite of our Biblical understanding of reality.

et's start our tour of the Greek gods with the most revered and famous of their deities – the goddess Athena, for whom Athens, Greece was named and whose forty-foot-tall gold and ivory statue dominated the Parthenon, atop the highest place in the ity. An exact-size replica of this statue was reconstructed for the model Parthenon in Nashville, TN (shown to the left). Note he statue's distorted inferences to the Biblical Eve – a snake at her side (as her counselor and companion); the head of Gorgon Medusa (the serpent) on her chest (as her guiding influence); Nike (symbolizing victory) resting in her hand (indicating the ictory she "won" for humanity when she ate the forbidden fruit); winged griffins (the head of a woman with the winged body f a lion) on her helmet (indicating power over heaven and Earth for the first woman); and a spear by her side (indicating the piritual defeat of God-fearing Noah and his sons). Throughout Greek art, various aspects of these symbols are always shown vith Athena in various scenes acting out these Biblical (albeit distorted) events.[1] Even Athena's name is a reference to the real Eve ho, because of the genetic purity of early mankind lived, *"god-like,"* for over 900 years (assuming she lived as long as Adam). In ncient Greek, death was written as *"thanas."* Athana literally means *"the deathless one,"* and the early form of the Goddess Athena vas written *"Athana"*[2]. It is quite obvious that the Biblical account of Adam and Eve were well known to the originators of Greek mythology and they borrowed, distorted, and re-worked these known istories of mankind to promote their own human-centered eligious beliefs.

GREECE

Greek Gods in Genesis?

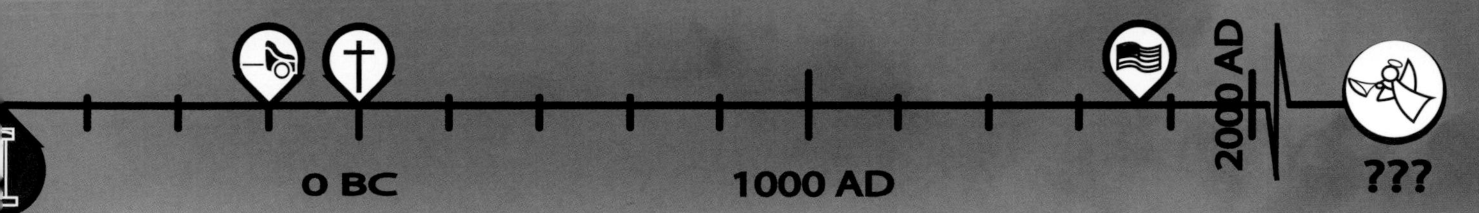

Although this page does not have room to document all the knowledge the Greeks had of the original human patriarchs, a brief summary comparing their mythology and the Genesis account is very revealing.
In Greek mythology, *Zeus and Hera* (recast after the flood as *Athena*) were the first couple from whom humans ultimately came. This couple lived in an original paradise called *the garden of Hesperides*, which is characterized as a place of soft light, gold for the taking, perfect health, and wondrous beauty. Depictions of the paradise painted on vases often show a serpent wound around an apple tree. *Zeus* is almost always shown holding a lightning bolt. The Greeks worshipped *Zeus* as the one who brought illumination to mankind. From the Greek viewpoint, Adam and Eve received the serpent's enlightenment and shared that enlightenment (symbolized by lightning) with all mankind.[1]

Just as Adam has two surviving sons named in Genesis (Cain and Seth), *Zeus* has two sons in Greek mythology – *Hephaistos* (the god of the forge – note that Cain's offspring were the first to become forgers of metal in Genesis 4:22) and *Ares* (considered worthless and even "pestilent" to the Greeks). Notice the Greek mythology twists everything backwards. The murderous Cain is elevated to hero status, while the God-honoring Seth is considered worthless in their belief system. Yet because he is an actual historical figure he still shows up in their mythology.

Noah is one of the most important figures in all human history because it is Noah from whom all humanity sprang after the flood and it is Noah who obeyed God and brought humanity through the world-restructuring flood. This event would not be forgotten by the ancient Greeks. One figure in Greek mythology is easily recognized on vases and sculptures because he is always holding a fish, portrayed beside a fish, or drawn having a fish tail. The Greeks called this figure *Nereus*, but it is interesting to note that he is the opposite of the Noah from the Bible. Although obviously revered for his knowledge, he is portrayed as passive and impotent. In various scenes in literature and artwork, Noah is shown to be under attack by *Herakles* (the great warrior and hunter – most likely representing the offspring of Noah's rebellious son Ham -- Nimrod), who takes Noah's sign of power from him – his trident – and gives it to the Greek god of the sea – *Poseidon*. This theme continues throughout Greek art as *Zeus* takes his scepter, *Athena* takes his cloak, and Poseidon and the *Zeus*-worshipping *Peleus* take his daughters. The message to the Greek people is unmistakable: Those who rebelled against the creator God (Adam and Eve, Cain, Ham, Nimrod, and their offspring) are the heroes who serve the serpent (and the "enlightenment" which he brings), while those who serve the old ways (by honoring a creator God) are powerless and defeated. This message can be seen on their art and sculptures, culminating in detailed stories told in almost 100 carved marble panels surrounding the top roofline of the Parthenon.

Greek culture started to develop over 3000 years ago completely independent of Hebrew culture, which recorded the most detailed, logical, and accurate account of the pattriarchs of mankind in Genesis chapters 1-11. The Greek's mythology is actually a record (although distorted) of exactly the same people and events mentioned in Genesis, and is an incredibly strong confirmation of the reality of these people and events.

GREECE

Whisper-Quiet Ancient Amphitheaters

Ancient amphitheaters have astounded researchers with their incredible acoustics. These massive civic centers can be found throughout the ancient Greek and Roman world -- holding up to 30,000 people and used for everything from ancient stage dramas and public speeches to gladiator fights. Yet people in the top row of these outdoor amphitheaters could hear actors or orators talking in a normal tone of voice (often hundreds of feet from the stage surface) nearly as well as those sitting in the front row.

The theater shown in the background of this page was built at Epidaurus, Greece during the 4th century B.C. It is arranged in fifty-five semi-circular rows, holding an estimated audience of 14,000. The incredible acoustics of this theater have been the source of academic and amateur speculation for many years, with theories attempting to explain the phenomenal acoustics ranging from the shape of the theater to suggestions that prevailing winds carried sounds upward or masked distracting sounds from the audience. It turns out that one key is actually the design of the seats![1]

Researchers at the Georgia Institute of Technology have discovered that the limestone seats provide a filtering effect – suppressing the low frequency of voices (thus minimizing background crowd breathing and movement noises) while reflecting higher-frequency sounds towards the audience (thus enhancing the vocal sounds coming from the stage). The slope of the theater also enhances this effect. Experiments with ultrasonic waves and numerical models indicated that frequencies up to 500 hertz are lowered (both from the stage and the surround ing audience) while frequencies higher than 500 hertz go undiminished. The corrugations on the surface of the

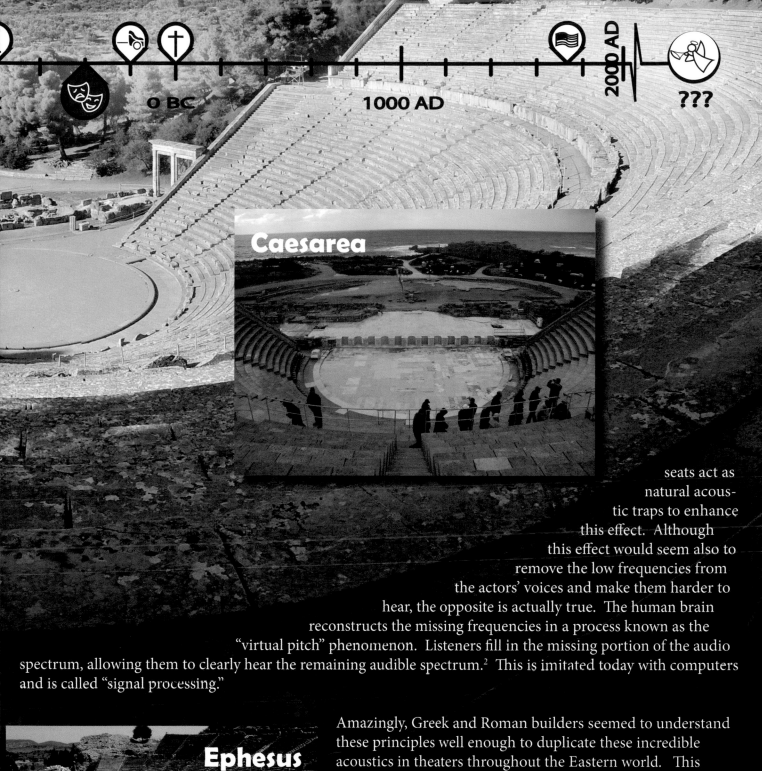

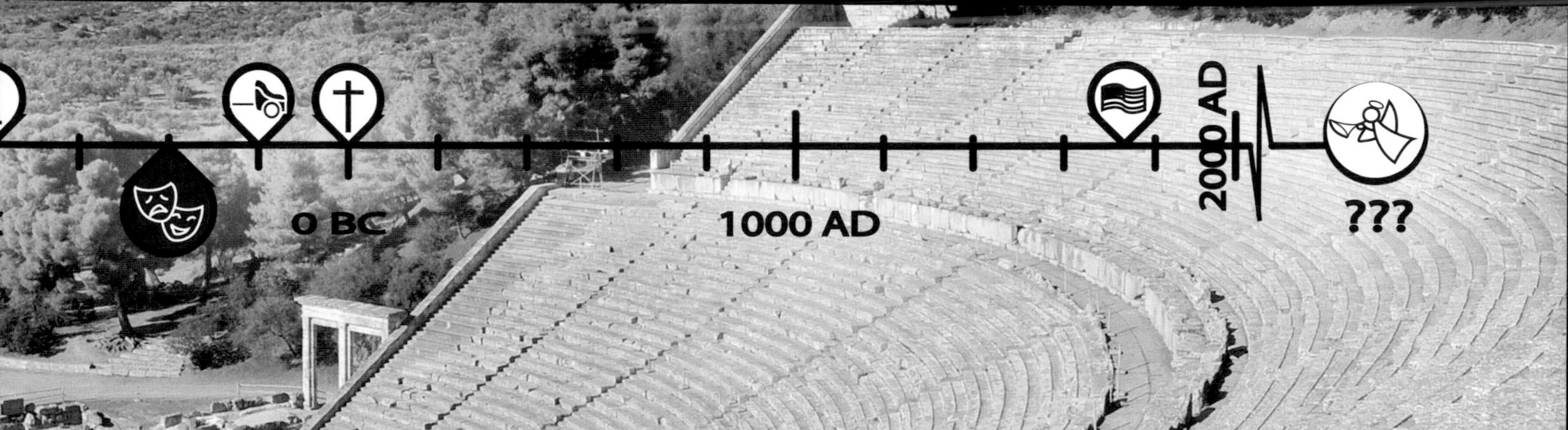

0 BC
1000 AD
2000 AD
???

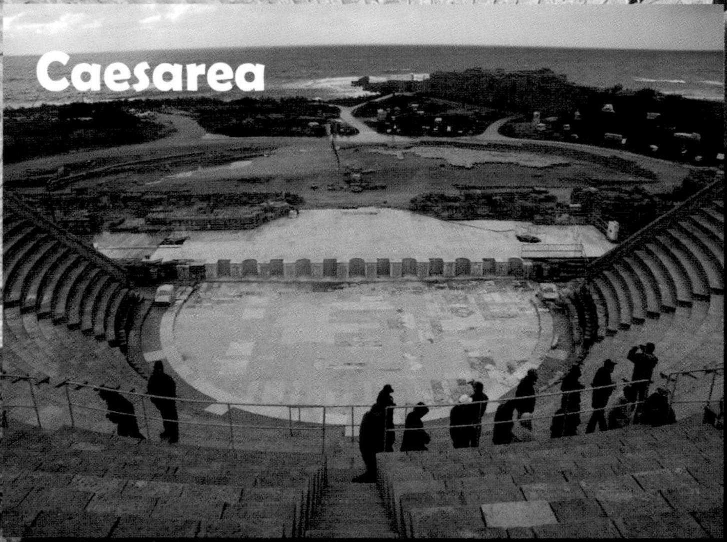

Caesarea

seats act as natural acoustic traps to enhance this effect. Although this effect would seem also to remove the low frequencies from the actors' voices and make them harder to hear, the opposite is actually true. The human brain reconstructs the missing frequencies in a process known as the "virtual pitch" phenomenon. Listeners fill in the missing portion of the audio spectrum, allowing them to clearly hear the remaining audible spectrum.[2] This is imitated today with computers and is called "signal processing."

Ephesus

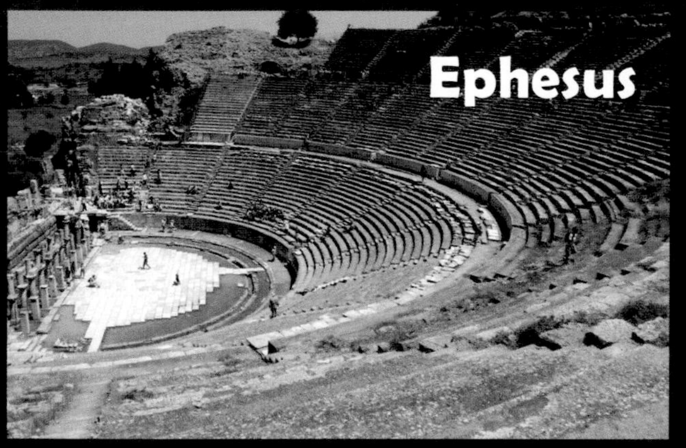

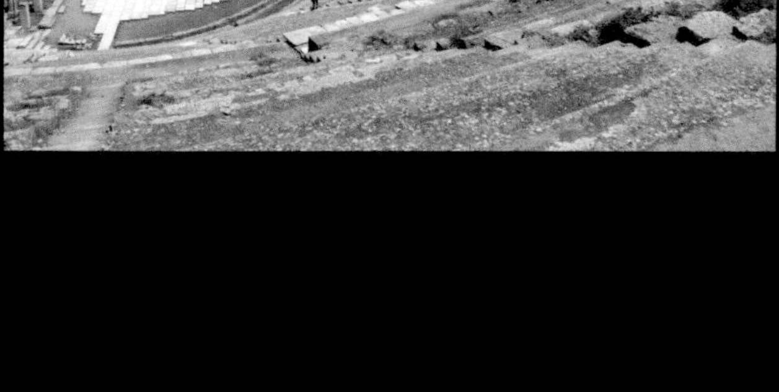

Amazingly, Greek and Roman builders seemed to understand these principles well enough to duplicate these incredible acoustics in theaters throughout the Eastern world. This knowledge was later lost as European theaters were built with other designs and wooden seats, which did not have nearly the acoustical perfection of the original ancient Greek and Roman theaters.

TURKEY
ISRAEL
GREECE

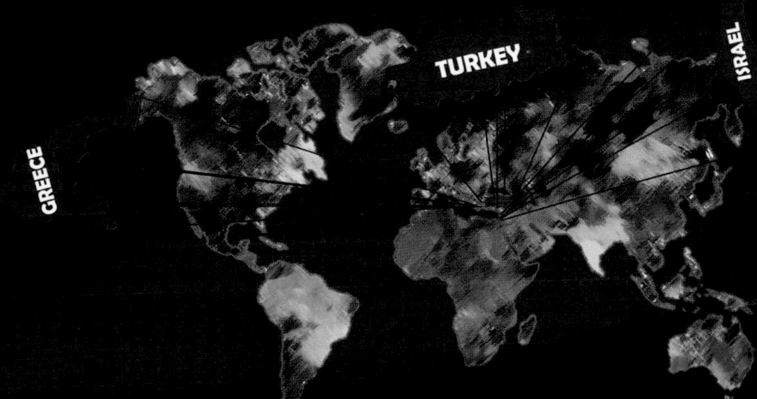

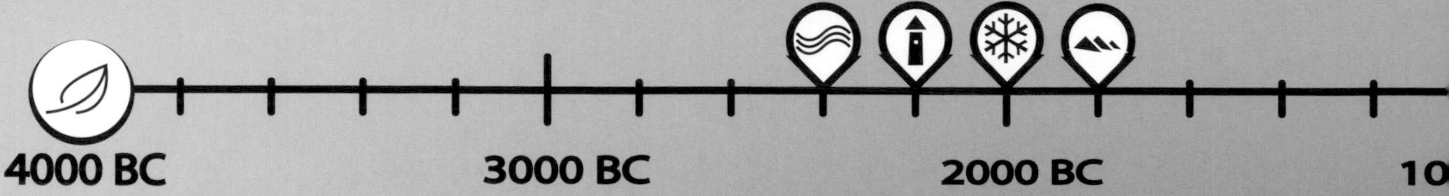

Ask your typical man-on-the-street what profession epitomizes human genius and you are likely to hear "rocket scientist" or "brain surgeon." It is truly amazing how rapidly modern science has developed our understanding and capability of dealing with medical problems. In only the last two hundred years medical knowledge has advanced from doctors as glorified barbers who routinely bled patients to MRI imaging (invented by Dr. Raymond Damadian – a young Earth creationist and Institute for Creation Research board member) and laser microsurgery. Yet as King Solomon noted 2500 years ago, *"There is nothing new under the sun"* (Ecclesiastes 1:9). Even our ability to extend human life spans is quite limited.

We assume that modern medical advances are responsible for a greatly extended human life span. In reality, we have lost medical knowledge that the ancients practiced and are barely keeping up with the rapidly deteriorating human body and ever-increasing maladies attacking us from within (genetic mistakes) and without (new virus and bacterial strains). The Bible records that humans routinely lived 800 or more years early in human history (6000 years ago). After the flood of Noah (4350 years ago), life spans dropped precipitately to about 400 years. By the time of Moses (3300 years ago), Psalm 90:10 notes that the life of man is seventy, maybe eighty, years, indicating that perhaps Moses was observing the shortening of man's lifespan. Today many people in undeveloped nations have an average life span of fifty-five years.[1] Without the re-discovery of antibiotics and "modern" medicine, we would be far behind even the ancient Peruvians in our ability to keep people alive.

Ancient Peruvian doctors were actually quite skilled at many types of surgery - including brain surgery! Ancient medical tool kits containing surgical knives made from sharpened obsidian stones have been shown to cut through human skin better than modern surgical steel scalpels - leaving less tearing and damage to the surrounding skin and muscle tissue.[2] Dozens of skulls have been found with holes ranging from 0.5 to 2 inches in diameter which have been cut or scraped through the skull. Apparently these surgeries were performed to correct a variety of maladies, from brain tumors to migraines. Many of these skulls show bone regrowth or a fusing of the bone to a metal plate - indicating that the patients lived for many years after the operation. How could these ancient people have developed such advanced medical knowledge?

Holes in your Head: Ancient Brain Surgery

It is pure cultural arrogance to assume that, just because we have made enormous medical advances, ancient cultures did not have their own areas of brilliant technological achievements. Ancient civilizations' knowledge of herbs and drugs is studied by modern scientists because these ancient doctors understood the use of

sedatives, anesthesia, and pain killers. Brain surgery using sharp obsidian knives to scraped circular openings in the skull, and cauterizing blood vessels to stop the flow of blood using pressure, heat, or medicines would not have been difficult. These surgeries may have been performed for spiritual or religious purposes. It is known today that external stimulation of certain parts of the brain can bring on dreams or revive long lost memories.[3] Those ancient doctors were experimenting with medical practices, which we have only recently "re-discovered." These discoveries reinforce what the Bible has taught for thousands of years - people have been made in God's image, and thus from the very beginning they have been intelligent, inquisitive, and inventive.

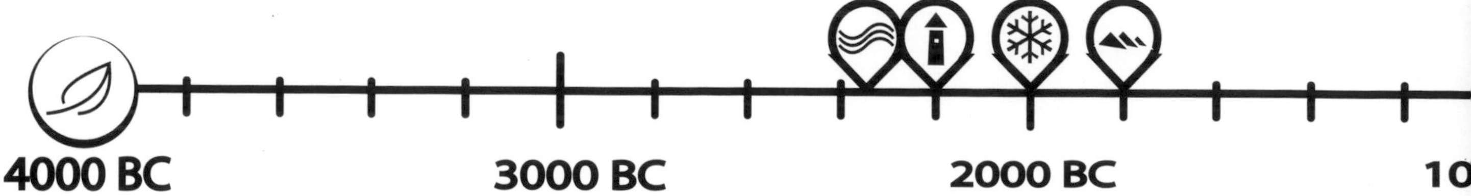

A Charge from Ancient History

Perhaps the defining feature of the modern world is mankind's ability to generate and use electricity. Without electricity there would be no modern communication, and it would still require months to get a message from one part of the world to another. Without electricity there would be no computers, televisions, video games, or cell phones. Millions employed by those industries would be idled, and the storage/transfer of knowledge would be slowed to a snail's pace. Electric motors would be gone. Refrigeration would be gone. Automobiles, trucks, trains, and airplanes would be gone. Travel into space is impossible without electronic circuitry. Modern dentistry, surgery, and lighting – all gone. We would go back to horses and wagons for moving goods; pulling teeth instead of filling cavities; leeches in place of operations; and candles in place of light bulbs. The world as we know it would essentially come to a grinding halt.

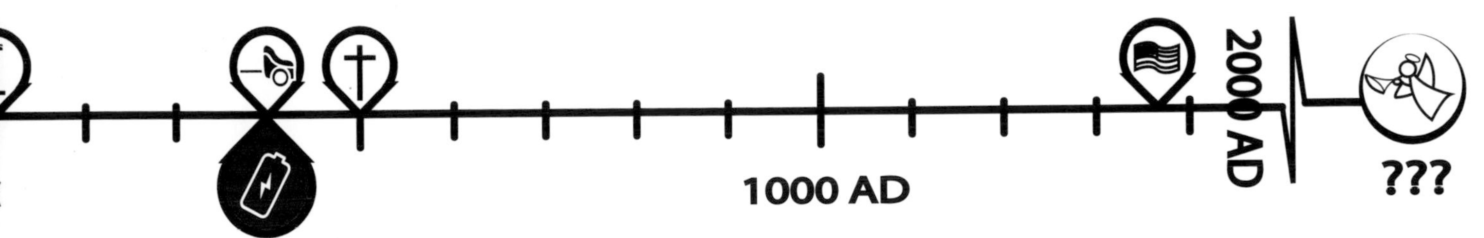

A convincing case can be made that it was the harnessing of electricity, only a few hundred years ago, which defines modern humanity. But was this ability really discovered only a few hundred years ago?

Multiple examples of working batteries, which date from ancient Iraq 2200 or more years ago, have been unearthed near Baghdad.[1,2] These artifacts have a post, sealed at the top and extending down into a clay vessel, which is surrounded by a copper cylinder. When filled with vinegar – or any other electrolytic solution -- the jar produces one to two volts. This is the essence of a working battery. Although controversial, it seems quite reasonable that ancient Mesopotamians discovered, generated, stored, and used electricity over 2000 years ago.

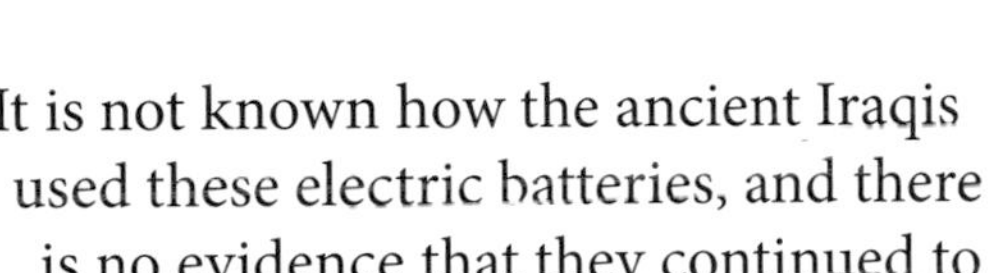

It is not known how the ancient Iraqis used these electric batteries, and there is no evidence that they continued to develop and harness knowledge in this area. Given the volatile nature of this region, with continual conflict and wars, it is not unlikely that the technology was simply forgotten without further developmental activity. Speculation of use for these batteries ranges from magician curiosities to gold removal from impure silver coins[3] to electroplating. Artifacts have been found with extremely thin metal coatings throughout the Middle East from Egypt to Turkey, supporting the possibility that electroplating techniques were both widespread and used even earlier than 2200 years ago. Given the small voltage potential of the battery, electroplating is the most likely usage, but this would require linking multiple cells together. The popular Mythbusters[tm] show got on board and confirmed that electroplating was, indeed, a possibility using these types of ancient batteries.[4] But the bigger perspective is the realization that the very knowledge that defines the modern age – the use of electricity – seems to have been developed by mankind over 2000 years ago!

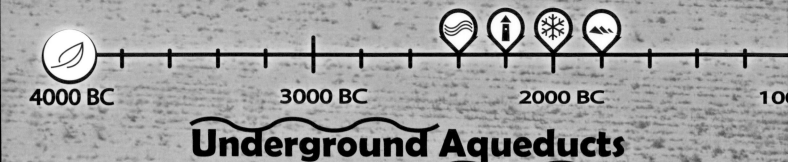

4000 BC 3000 BC 2000 BC 100

Underground Aqueducts

Water. All living things on Earth are dependent upon water. Human bodies are composed of sixty percent water. We might survive up to sixty days without food, but will die within six days without water. Mankind has invented imaginative methods of moving water for crops, drinking, and sanitation, but perhaps none is so inventive as the underwater aqueduct systems found at Cantayo in Nazca, Peru and ancient Mesopotamia (Iraq).

Over 2,000 years ago, in pre-Inca times, the inhabitants of Nazca developed a system of underground aqueducts to irrigate dry lands that lacked surface water. In this area there is a wide, dry river bed, which apparently carried abundant water through the region during the wetter period of Earth history known as the Ice Age (3600 - 4200 years ago). Following the Ice Age, rainfall around the world tapered off, ground water table levels dropped, and the stream beds dried up – leaving this region of Peru an arid desert. What were the residents to do? Inventive engineers dug a series of spiral open manholes, as much as thirty feet deep, down to the water table, which still exists well below the ancient riverbed. They then burrowed tunnels between these "open manholes," lined the entire underground channel with stones, and created a unique underground aqueduct to carry water from this underground water reservoir to lower-level farm fields (located thousands

of feet away from the dried river bed). Once out in the open fields, the water was diverted into channels to water their crops. Pictured on this page are two converging arms of the aqueduct, which feed a single larger arm of the underground aqueduct – bringing life-giving water to the surrounding fields located out of the picture to the right.

In spite of the harshness of the desert, farmers in the Nazca region still use over thirty of these ancient underground channels, originally constructed over 2000 years ago, to grow cotton, corn, beans, potatoes, and a wide variety of fruit. Can you imagine any sewer system built by modern man which would still be functional 2000 years from now? Most modern systems need to be rebuilt every few decades.

Even older are the underground aqueducts bringing water from the Euphrates and Tigris Rivers to arid lands in Iraq. Iraq is one of the oldest civilizations on Earth. These people calculated the exact slope needed in their aqueducts, such that the resulting water flow was not too fast (which would cause erosion) or too slow (which would allow sediment to settle and clog the channel). They then dug manholes down at regular intervals and tunneled between the manholes to create the first-ever underground aqueduct.

The inventiveness of both Peruvian and Mesopotamian engineers testifies to the genius of those who constructed these marvels of ancient engineering.

PERU

ART FOR ALIENS

Imagine creating a work of art with no expectation of anyone ever seeing or appreciating it. In addition, your masterpiece would be so large that it would require the help of dozens of people, be spread over hundreds of acres of land, and take thousands of man-hours to complete. Furthermore, you would need to move millions of pounds of rocks and have to produce perfectly placed lines and curves without even being able to see the final result as you worked. Even with today's laser and surveying technologies, the job would be a challenge. Thousands of years ago such an accomplishment would have been unthinkable. Yet, this is exactly what the people of ancient Peru achieved - not just once but with dozens of massive artworks and geometric figures.

Two hundred miles south of Lima, ancient people of the Nazca area moved rocks and rubble from the desert floor in order to produce works of art which extended as far as nine miles in perfectly straight lines, thereby creating images of spiders, hummingbirds, trees, pelicans, foxes, and other animals. The animal outlines are as large as three football fields in length and can only be vaguely seen at low angles from the surrounding hills. But all of these geoglyphs are clearly visible from airplanes flying overhead. This has given alien

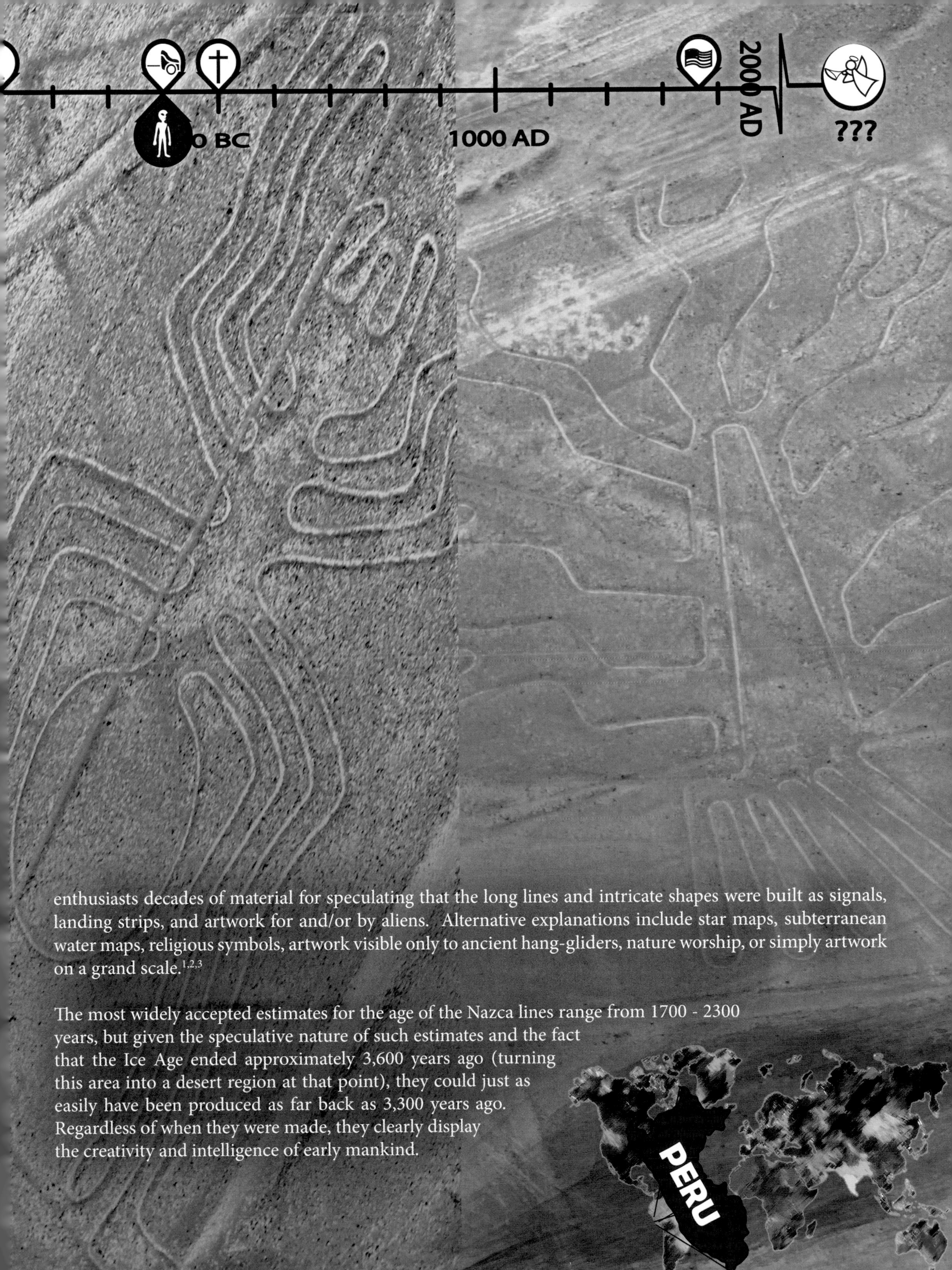

enthusiasts decades of material for speculating that the long lines and intricate shapes were built as signals, landing strips, and artwork for and/or by aliens. Alternative explanations include star maps, subterranean water maps, religious symbols, artwork visible only to ancient hang-gliders, nature worship, or simply artwork on a grand scale.[1,2,3]

The most widely accepted estimates for the age of the Nazca lines range from 1700 - 2300 years, but given the speculative nature of such estimates and the fact that the Ice Age ended approximately 3,600 years ago (turning this area into a desert region at that point), they could just as easily have been produced as far back as 3,300 years ago. Regardless of when they were made, they clearly display the creativity and intelligence of early mankind.

Army of the Dead

One of the characteristics of all human cultures is the acknowledgement of life after death. All cultures from the ancient Egyptians to Neanderthals - from the Aborigines to ancient Chinese - have buried their loved ones with useful artifacts in the hope that the dead could use these items in their life after death. In reality, we will bring nothing into eternity (except others to whom we have had the privilege of explaining that eternal life with God comes only through acceptance of salvation through Jesus). But the very fact that all cultures have the need to prepare for the afterlife testifies to the universal knowledge that God put into the consciousness of all humanity - that our life does not end at physical death. One astounding testimony to both the ability and skill of ancient humans, AND the strength of their belief in the afterlife, can be found in central China.

The first emperor to unify China under a single dynasty was named Qin Shi Huang Di (260 BC - 210 BC), and although he reigned for only twenty-six years, in that time he started the modernization of China's Great Wall; standardized China's writing, currency, and measurement systems; and constructed a thirty-five-acre complex for his own tomb, which included approximately 9000 life-sized terra cotta (clay) soldiers, horses, magicians, and acrobats. The terra cotta army figures were manufactured by government laborers in workshops by molding the head, arms, legs, and torsos separately and then assembling the body before firing it in large ovens. Eight different face molds were used and individual facial features added such that all the individuals in the army had their own unique appearance. Each workshop was even required to inscribe its name on the mass-produced items to ensure quality control.

Most of the figures originally held actual weapons such as swords, spears, battle-axes, scimitars, shields, and crossbows. A few figures still hold weapons, but most seem to be missing and are thought to have been looted shortly after the creation of the army or rotted away (if made of wood).[1] Upon completion, the terra cotta figures were painted with vibrant, bright colors. The entire complex is being carefully dug out of wet, mud-like sediment, but once exposed to the dry air of the region, the paint on the figurines starts to curl, fade, and fall off within seconds.

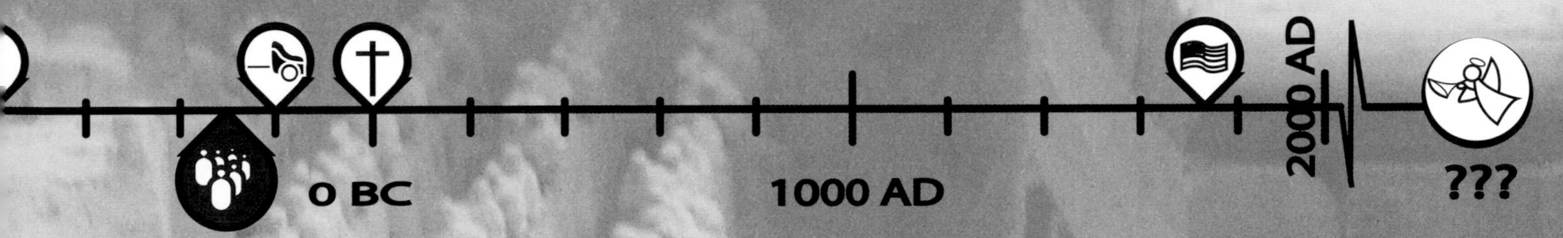

At present less than ten percent of the massive burial complex has been uncovered, but it is believed to have been originally constructed in only a few years, using a labor force of 700,000 workers![2,3] Compare this to the number of people working for NASA from 1963 - 1972 on the six Apollo missions to send men to the moon – approximately 400,000. The brilliance and ability of mankind has not changed – only the focus of his projects and the technology used. Imagine the artistic skill, organizational ability, labor management, ingenuity, and attention to detail needed to pull off a project of this magnitude with a labor force of that size. These skills did not instantly appear from nowhere. Skills such as these must have been present for many generations previous to the colossal achievement in order for the emperor to start such an ambitious project. Thus, within a thousand or so years of the flood, people were already developing the skills needed to achieve such massive building projects and artistic accomplishments.

CHINA

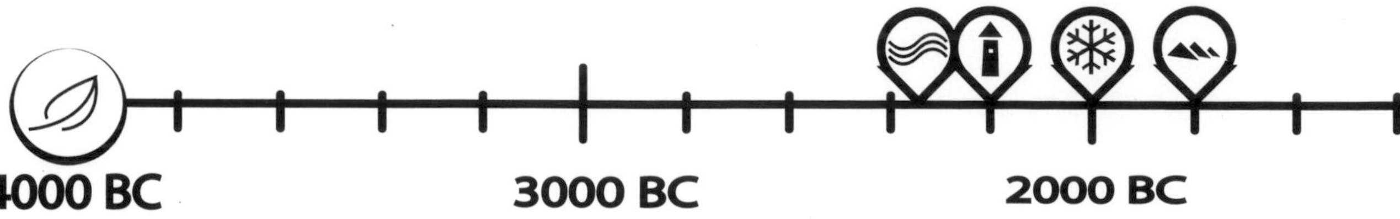

But it's "JUST" paper

Sometimes it is the simple things which change everything. Take paper, for instance. It is such a fixture in our everyday existence that we forget what life would be like without it. Electronic communication is still an EXTREMELY recent development. Without paper having been invented first, it is unlikely knowledge would have advanced to the degree that electronics would ever have been invented. Without paper we would be reduced to transferring and retaining information on animal skins, tree bark, or clay tablets. If you ever tried to transcribe complex information onto papyrus, clay tablets, or leather scrolls, you would immediately understand why simple paper is a godsend.

Without paper we would not have books, cheap boxes with which to transport goods, colorful wall coverings, mail service, wrapping paper, calendars, printing, photographs, printed money, many building materials, blueprints, pencils, much of our artwork, most product packaging, the development of plastics (as a paper replacement likely would not have happened), absorbent paper towels, diapers, or a multitude of other modern conveniences. And let's not forget about toilet paper! One could make the case that the advancement of modern man's technology is closely tied to his widespread development of paper manufacturing operations in the 1300s.

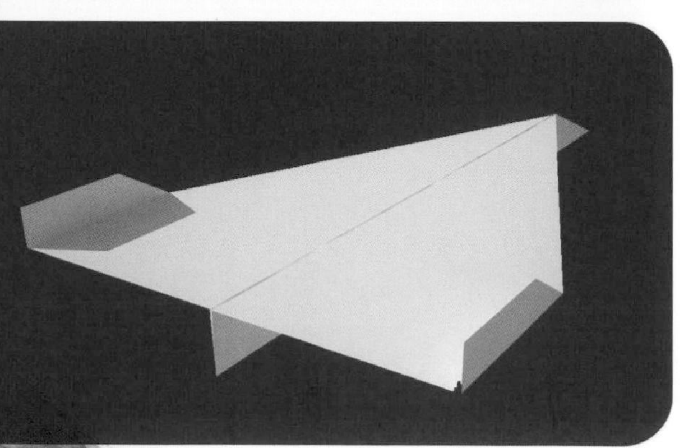

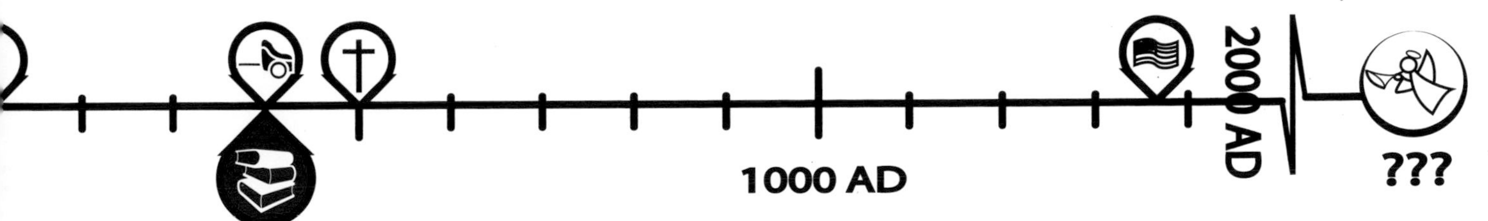

Paper manufacturing first came to Europe in the 12th century - having slowly come westward via trade routes from the Orient.[1] The arrogant attitude of much history education implies that mankind is far more evolved than earlier humans (who were busy wiping each other out during the iron age, bronze age, stone age, and before). And when we weren't busy killing each other, people were being wiped out by various forms of ignorance such as poor sanitation (which wiped out one-third of the population of Europe in the 1300s). In other words, it wasn't until the development of modern science (which corresponded to the widespread use of paper as a medium to spread knowledge) that mankind was able to advance. In reality, paper, in all its forms and uses, was not invented by the Western world 800 years ago, but was invented in China at least 1500 years earlier.

China has been manufacturing and using paper for writing, artwork, decorations, wrapping materials, transporting of goods, building materials, and intricately folded three-dimensional shapes for at least 2200 years. The earliest samples of Chinese paper were found in the tomb of Emperor Wu, who reigned in 140 BC, but the use of paper may go back even further. Later nobles and ruling class Chinese sent paper letters to friends and folded them into intricate shapes – thereby inventing the art of origami. Even before the widespread use of paper, written documents were organized into collections for safekeeping - the earliest private collection of ancient Chinese writings (i.e. libraries) discovered so far dates from 2550 years ago.[2] The first known written dictionary was also in China - written on paper 1900 years ago by an early philologist named Xu Shen. The Chinese use of ink writing even predates paper, going back to the very beginnings of civilization after the flood - with ink characters written on bone, approximately 4000 years ago.

CHINA

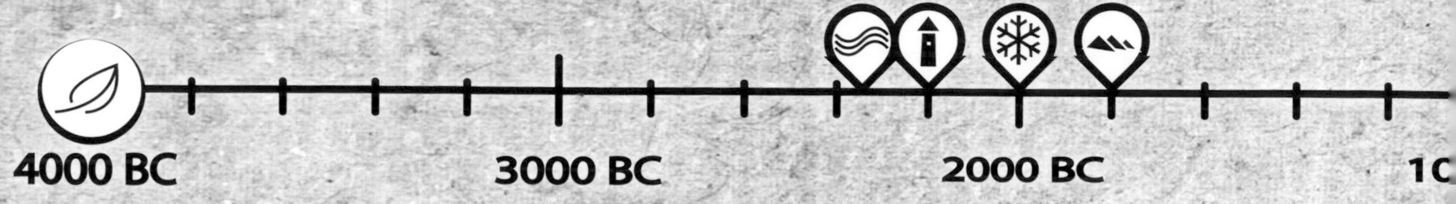

Library of Alexandria

As both the depth and breadth of the knowledge of mankind exploded after the establishment of cultures following the worldwide flood, the need to document, preserve, and transfer this knowledge from one generation to the next became a challenge. Complex written languages had been created in cultures across the world, but systematically capturing the ideas, history, and technology of these cultures in such a way that these things would not be forgotten became an increasing challenge. It can be argued that prior to a few hundred years ago, more history and knowledge has been lost than retained in the mists of time.

One culture's attempt to prevent this loss of knowledge is notable in both its magnitude and implementation – the Library of Alexandria. This ancient depository of human knowledge was built 2300 years ago in proximity to Alexandria, Egypt. Many of the most influential thinkers of the ancient world came to this complex to study, and the entire area functioned as an ancient precursor to our modern universities. Although paper had been invented by China about the same time, paper manufacturing had not yet reached the West, and books were still compiled as written scrolls on animal skins, thin metal plates, or papyrus paper. Even though all of these involved the laborious handwritten transfer of knowledge from one document to the next and were bulky documents compared to the amount of information contained

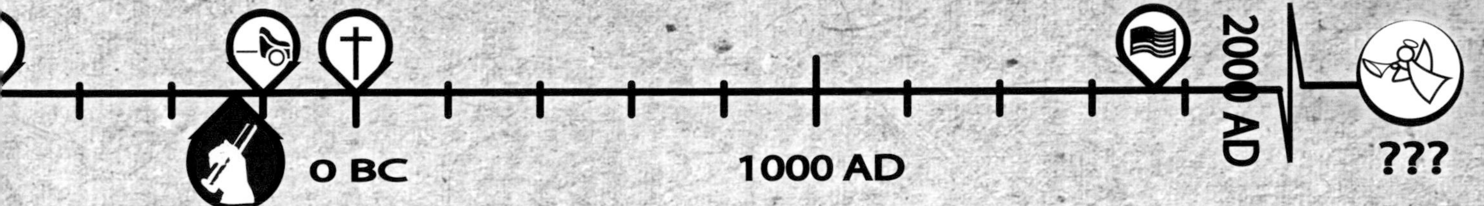

in a book (with its thin paper pages), this library contained an enormous wealth of ancient knowledge on mathematics, astronomy, physics, natural sciences, philosophy, history, religion, and many other subjects. The Library of Alexandria was famous throughout the ancient world as a depository of knowledge and is referred to in numerous ancient historical documents[1]. It was believed to contain over a million scrolls. Mark Antony was even reported to have taken the 200,000 scrolls from the great Library of Pergamum and donated them to the Library of Alexandria as a wedding gift to Cleopatra.

The mere size of this magnificent collection of human knowledge, from cultures since the reestablishment of mankind's foothold upon the globe only 2000 years earlier, testifies to the genius and industriousness of mankind. Tragically, essentially all of the library's scrolls were destroyed by invasions and fires in 48 BC, 279 AD, and 391 AD. Fragments and references to knowledge from the library still surface from time to time - such as the information needed to produce the 1519 Piri Reis map of the non-ice-covered Antarctic coastline (page 44).

This knowledge likely came from explorers traveling the world during the Ice Age (3600 - 4200 years ago) when the ocean levels were lower, and the Antarctic ocean waters were still significantly warmer following Noah's Flood. The information for the Piri Reis map must have found its way from earlier civilizations to the Library of Alexandria, and ultimately survived to be copied by an Italian map maker in the 16th century. The Library of Alexandria is an ancient wonder testifying to the brilliance of mankind.

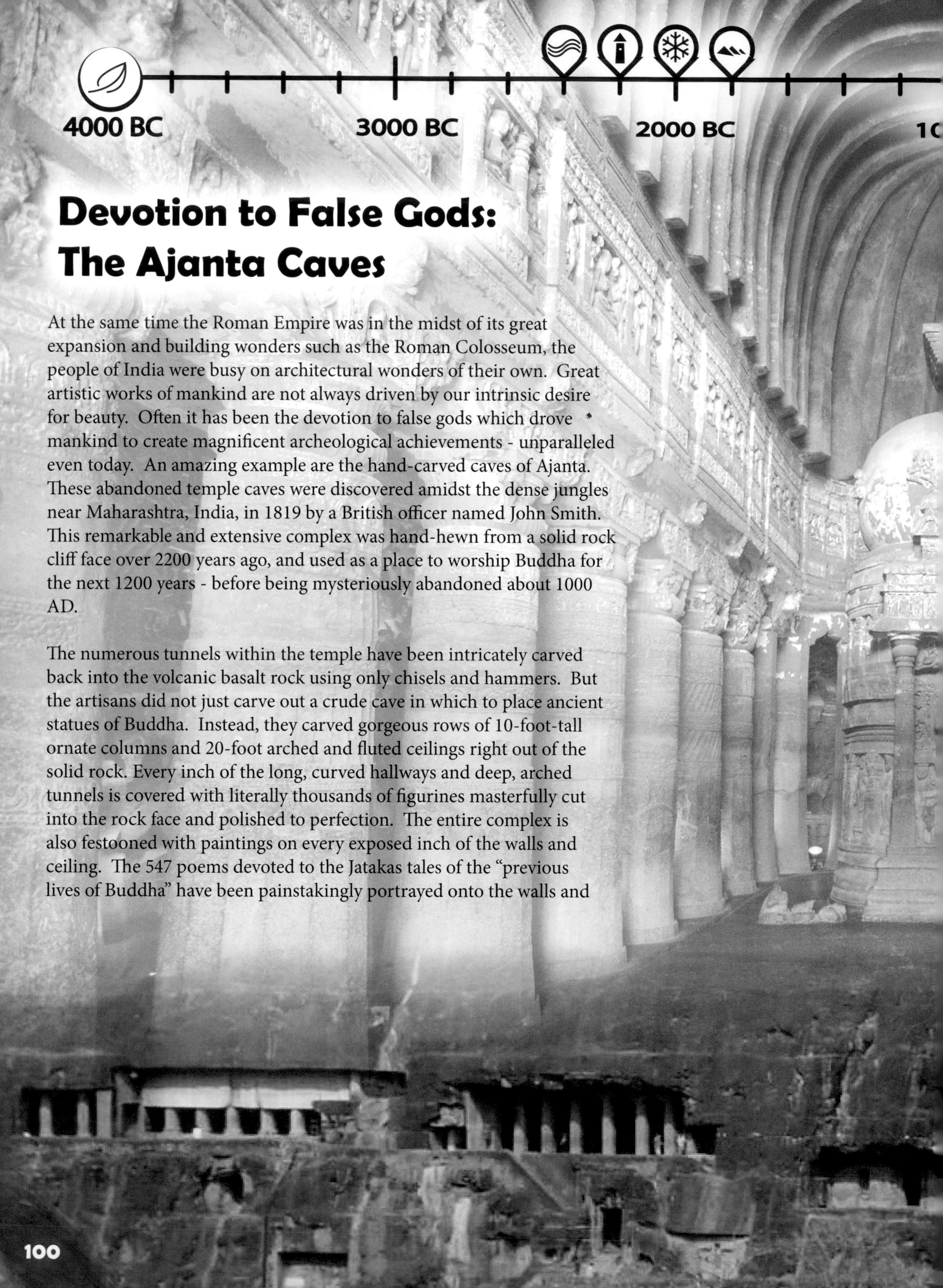

Devotion to False Gods: The Ajanta Caves

At the same time the Roman Empire was in the midst of its great expansion and building wonders such as the Roman Colosseum, the people of India were busy on architectural wonders of their own. Great artistic works of mankind are not always driven by our intrinsic desire for beauty. Often it has been the devotion to false gods which drove mankind to create magnificent archeological achievements - unparalleled even today. An amazing example are the hand-carved caves of Ajanta. These abandoned temple caves were discovered amidst the dense jungles near Maharashtra, India, in 1819 by a British officer named John Smith. This remarkable and extensive complex was hand-hewn from a solid rock cliff face over 2200 years ago, and used as a place to worship Buddha for the next 1200 years - before being mysteriously abandoned about 1000 AD.

The numerous tunnels within the temple have been intricately carved back into the volcanic basalt rock using only chisels and hammers. But the artisans did not just carve out a crude cave in which to place ancient statues of Buddha. Instead, they carved gorgeous rows of 10-foot-tall ornate columns and 20-foot arched and fluted ceilings right out of the solid rock. Every inch of the long, curved hallways and deep, arched tunnels is covered with literally thousands of figurines masterfully cut into the rock face and polished to perfection. The entire complex is also festooned with paintings on every exposed inch of the walls and ceiling. The 547 poems devoted to the Jatakas tales of the "previous lives of Buddha" have been painstakingly portrayed onto the walls and

ceiling by the ancient artists. Although time has taken its toll upon these marvelous works due to centuries of weathering (the caves are open to the air and were home to birds, bats, and other jungle animals for almost a thousand years), many fragments of the original works are still colorful and complete. How could any of these paintings have survived so long when open to the elements? The artists started by chiseling the walls or ceiling to roughen the surface so that there would be an extremely strong bond between the rock surface and wet plaster which was spread onto the roughened surface. Then the master painter would commence his work while the plaster was still wet. His colors soaked into the plaster and became part of the bonded surface, rather than just a painted layer on top of the plaster surface. This method prevented the colors from easily fading or peeling off, but it is doubtful that even the painters foresaw their work enduring for over two thousand years.

These building and painting techniques no doubt extended much farther back into human history. The Ajanta caves are merely one of the grandest remaining examples of these abilities demonstrated by ancient mankind. The millions of man-hours and enormous effort required to create this ancient masterpiece of human engineering is indeed mindboggling. How sad that this expenditure of human life was devoted to a false, human-invented god instead of being dedicated to the Creator of all things. Perhaps this is why it was ultimately abandoned and forgotten.

The Ancient Peruvian Language

Stringing Together Words

Humans have a unique, God-given ability to communicate by assigning meaning to abstract symbols. This is commonly known as written language. Think about any written language - whether it's English, Chinese, or Egyptian hieroglyphics. The individual symbols (letters) are combined to form a larger grouping (words), which are combined in a way to communicate complex meanings (sentences or paragraphs). But each starting symbol must be assigned a meaning (and a sound if it is a spoken language), and the combination of symbols have to be assigned a mutually agreed-upon meaning so that the person initiating the communication can transfer the meaning to the person receiving the sequence of symbols.

The method of assigning meaning to symbols does not even have to be written. Think about the smoke signals of ancient Native Americans. The size and spacing of the smoke puffs were essentially writing in the air, just as a dash, dot, and space can be used to communicate using Morse Code. The ability to develop unique and complex forms of communication is one indication of the unique intelligence of humanity. From an evolutionary point of view, one would think that ancient man would have used a much simpler form of "written" communication, with languages having fewer letters, fewer verb tenses, and simpler symbols (i.e. less "degrees of freedom" in the written and verbal language). It turns out that the exact opposite is true. Early languages actually had more letters, more verb forms, and far more complexity than modern languages. In other words, the developers of the original human written languages were much more mentally advanced than most people today.

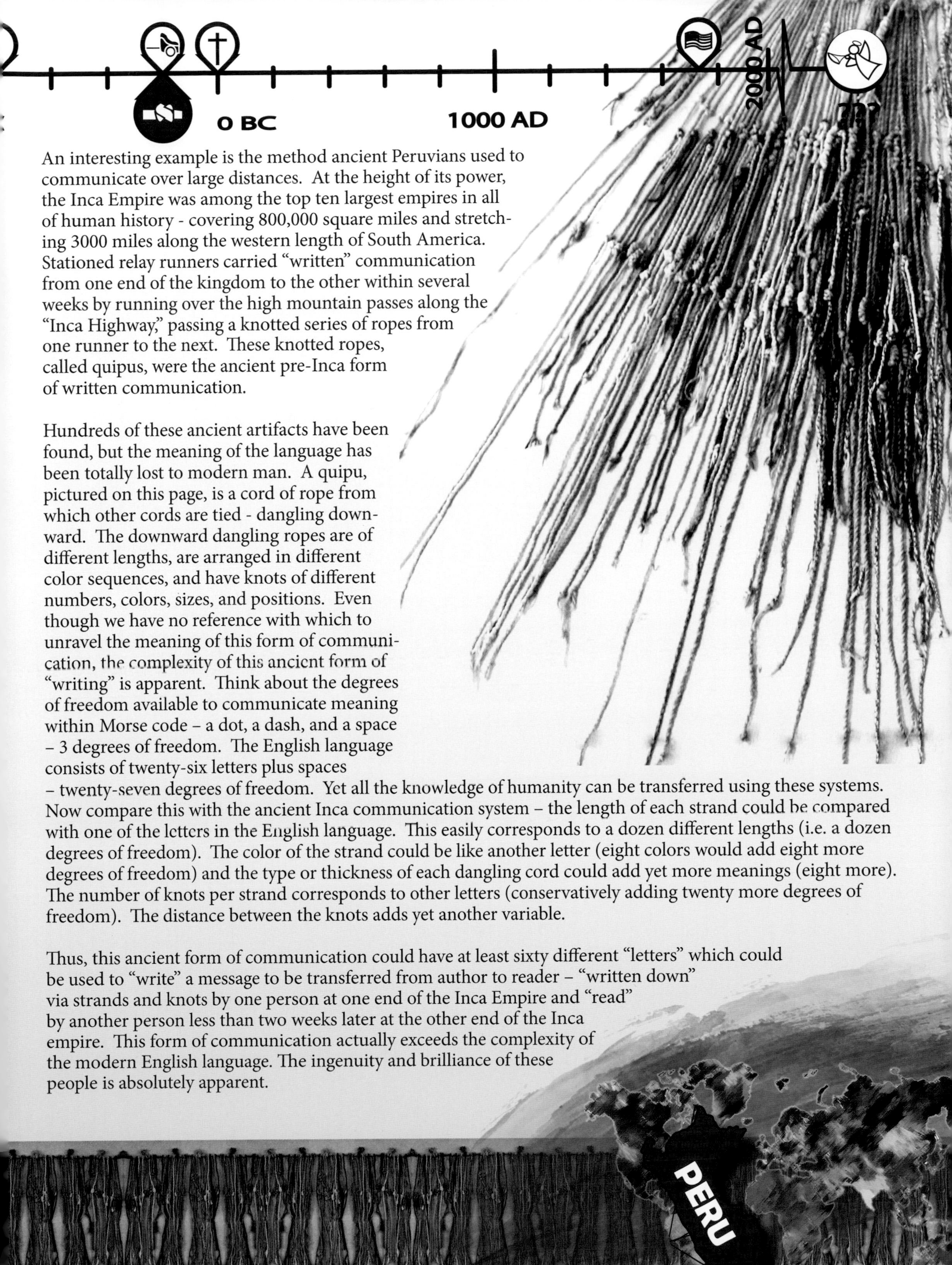

An interesting example is the method ancient Peruvians used to communicate over large distances. At the height of its power, the Inca Empire was among the top ten largest empires in all of human history - covering 800,000 square miles and stretching 3000 miles along the western length of South America. Stationed relay runners carried "written" communication from one end of the kingdom to the other within several weeks by running over the high mountain passes along the "Inca Highway," passing a knotted series of ropes from one runner to the next. These knotted ropes, called quipus, were the ancient pre-Inca form of written communication.

Hundreds of these ancient artifacts have been found, but the meaning of the language has been totally lost to modern man. A quipu, pictured on this page, is a cord of rope from which other cords are tied - dangling downward. The downward dangling ropes are of different lengths, are arranged in different color sequences, and have knots of different numbers, colors, sizes, and positions. Even though we have no reference with which to unravel the meaning of this form of communication, the complexity of this ancient form of "writing" is apparent. Think about the degrees of freedom available to communicate meaning within Morse code – a dot, a dash, and a space – 3 degrees of freedom. The English language consists of twenty-six letters plus spaces – twenty-seven degrees of freedom. Yet all the knowledge of humanity can be transferred using these systems. Now compare this with the ancient Inca communication system – the length of each strand could be compared with one of the letters in the English language. This easily corresponds to a dozen different lengths (i.e. a dozen degrees of freedom). The color of the strand could be like another letter (eight colors would add eight more degrees of freedom) and the type or thickness of each dangling cord could add yet more meanings (eight more). The number of knots per strand corresponds to other letters (conservatively adding twenty more degrees of freedom). The distance between the knots adds yet another variable.

Thus, this ancient form of communication could have at least sixty different "letters" which could be used to "write" a message to be transferred from author to reader – "written down" via strands and knots by one person at one end of the Inca Empire and "read" by another person less than two weeks later at the other end of the Inca empire. This form of communication actually exceeds the complexity of the modern English language. The ingenuity and brilliance of these people is absolutely apparent.

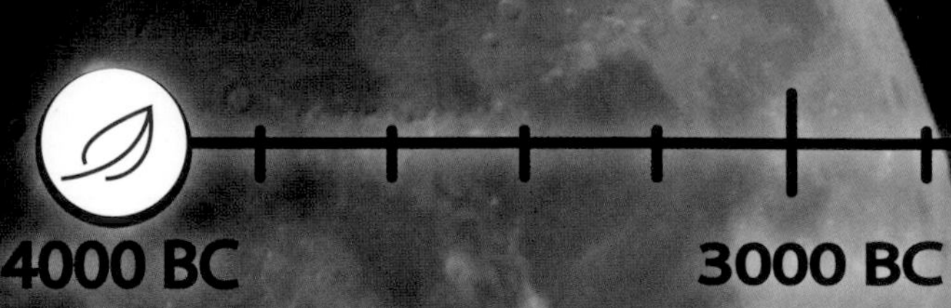

The Greek Computer

We tend to think of computers as purely digital data processing devices, but the original numerical calculators and computers were gear/lever-driven devices which tabulated numbers via moving parts. As electronics were invented, the mechanical parts were merely replaced by digital symbols for tallying columns and rows of numbers. The earliest machine which qualifies as a "computer-like" device, is the Antikythera mechanism, which was designed to calculate astronomical positions. This corroded and sediment-encrusted artifact was recovered from the Mediterranean Sea in multiple pieces from 1900 - 1901 but sat in a museum until 1971, when researchers took X-ray images of the eighty-two fragments. What they found was an intricate series of thirty bronze gears and levers perfectly designed, such that the movement of the sun, moon, and possibly the other five visible planets within our solar system could be predicted with perfect accuracy.[1]

Professor Michael Edmunds of Cardiff University, who led a 2006 study of the mechanism, summarized the significance of this find:

> *"This device is just extraordinary, the only thing of its kind. The design is beautiful, the astronomy is exactly right. The way the mechanics are designed just makes your jaw drop. Whoever has done this has done it extremely carefully ... in terms of historic and scarcity value, I have to regard this mechanism as being more valuable than the Mona Lisa."*[2]

So what makes this finding so significant? The fact that it was found within the wreckage of an ancient Greek cargo ship, which sank over 2100 years ago! Sponge divers retrieved numerous artifacts from the wreck, including bronze and marble statues, pottery, vases, glassware, jewelry, and coins, but none have the significance of this complex mechanism. It was not until 1,600 years later that mankind regained the ability to manufacture such finely crafted and interlocking metal gears for use in clocks, computational machines,

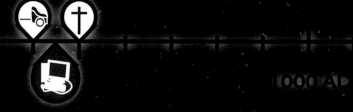

and other mechanical applications.[3] The implications of this find are staggering to our understanding of the capabilities of mankind.

First, it supports the reality that mankind has always possessed extreme intelligence. Metal work is mentioned as one of the abilities of mankind within several generations of mankind's creation (Genesis 4:22). Thus, the casting of metal into intricate shapes probably goes back for thousands of years prior to this mechanism. It is the incredible precision which sets this structure apart from many other bronze artifacts.

Second, this gear-making knowledge and ability was apparently lost 2100 years ago, only to be rediscovered about 500 years ago. This fact allows for the possibility that these same skills were known before the flood (4,400 years ago) only to be rediscovered 2100 years ago. A wide variety of knowledge has been lost for periods of time throughout history, only later to be re-invented or rediscovered. This testifies not to the evolving and increasing intelligence of mankind, but to the original brilliance of mankind.

Third, this find testifies to the ability of early man to study, understand, model, and predict natural processes such as the exact movement of the sun, moon, and planets. This is the essence of science – understanding how creation operates and using this understanding to predict (and ultimately harness) these natural processes. In other words, we often think that mankind's technology has grown over time - in spite of setbacks with previous technological advances being forgotten – but archeological finds such as the Antikytheral mechanism demonstrate that mankind has always possessed incredible intelligence and used it to develop advanced technology.

Rise of Science
2000 Years Ago to Modern Era

No one needs to be convinced that the modern world has achieved amazing advancements in technology. For that reason only a few examples of mankind's knowledge from early in this period will be highlighted. The primary purpose of this volume has been to demonstrate that even earlier generations of mankind were just as inventive and intelligent as recent generations, and many of the foundational principles of science were known and used by human beings very early in history.

In just the last few centuries, we have moved from locomotion by horse (essentially no different than 3,000 years earlier) to jet airplanes and spacecraft capable of traveling to the moon. We have advanced from laboriously duplicating written documents to almost instantaneously transmitting billions of pages of information and images anyplace in the world using electronic transmission via satellites. We've moved from wind

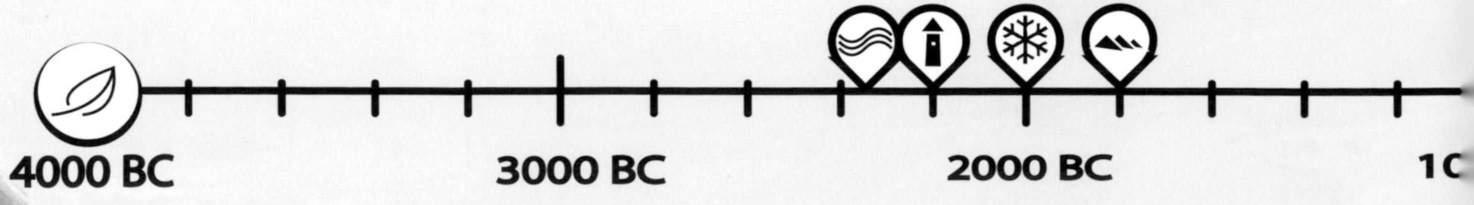

transportation to harnessing internal combustion engines and understanding the laws of nature, which allow for the development of refrigeration, atomic energy, and amazing medical advances. And the vast majority of this advancement in knowledge has taken place in the last 200 years.

For many people, modern science has replaced belief in the true God. Because we have become so adept at understanding "how creation operates" and proficient at using this knowledge to manipulate and control creation, arrogant modern man has increasingly come to believe that creation made itself. This is really just another form of the pagan worship of creation in place of an acknowledgment of our Creator. Forgotten is the fact that essentially all of the founders of modern science - men such as Newton, Faraday, Kelvin, Pasteur, Pascal, Maxwell, and others - were all Bible-believing Christians who acknowledged that the universe and life had been recently created by God. It was this confidence that there was a logical, intelligent, knowable Creator behind it all that gave them the confidence to study creation in a systematic way in order to advance the principles of modern science. Every one of our modern technologies (many of which were already being explored thousands of years earlier), is built upon a foundation laid down by others.

Had the founders of modern science not been men of faith who understood the distinction between operational science and the Divine Originator of science, modern science would never have developed. Only because there is an all-powerful, all-knowing (and logical) Creator God, are there discoverable physical laws of science which rule the universe. The random processes of evolution do not explain the supposed upward advancement of life nor do they explain the origin of the finely tuned laws of nature and science.

Firm Foundation

Near the ancient temple grounds in Baalbek, Lebanon, there remain buried two of the largest stones ever cut by mankind. The first, known as the "pregnant woman stone," was uncovered in the 1800s (pictured above) and is estimated to weigh 800 tons (1.6 million pounds). A second, similar-shaped monolith was uncovered nearby in the 1990s and is estimated to weigh 1200 tons (2.4 million pounds).

It is still hotly debated how these stones were quarried, when they were produced, and how they were moved. The nearby temple, built by the Romans during a 200-year period from 1900 - 2100 years ago, contains three enormous 500-ton rectangular stones (known as "*The Trilithon Stones*") which lay end-to-end along one narrow wall on the western end of the complex. It is acknowledged that the Romans built upon previous

ruins from civilizations going back almost 4000 years. Thus, many investigators believe that the large blocks are actually stones cut by a previous civilization, which the Romans used as their foundation when they built the newer temple complex.[1]

However, some of researchers firmly believe it was the Romans who quarried, moved, and laid all of the stones. They attribute the enormous monolithic stones near the base of the temple structure (weighing in excess of a million pounds each) to placement as a retaining wall along one side of the temple in order to prevent movement of earth in the nearby hillside from shifting the temple structure. They believe the massive blocks of granite were moved via pulleys, levers, rollers, and LOTS of manpower.[2] Yet the stones are not at the structure's foundation but several layers up.

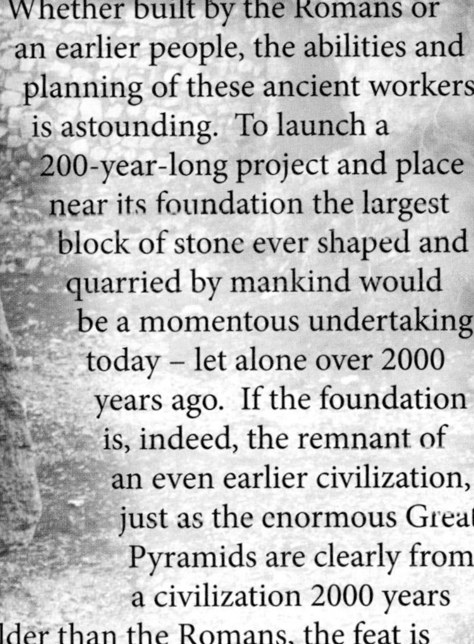

Whether built by the Romans or an earlier people, the abilities and planning of these ancient workers is astounding. To launch a 200-year-long project and place near its foundation the largest block of stone ever shaped and quarried by mankind would be a momentous undertaking today – let alone over 2000 years ago. If the foundation is, indeed, the remnant of an even earlier civilization, just as the enormous Great Pyramids are clearly from a civilization 2000 years older than the Romans, the feat is even more amazing.

The Trilithon Stones compared to people

4000 BC 3000 BC 2000 BC 10

The REAL Fake

Throughout this book, ancient Peruvian burial stones have been featured with images of dinosaurs, ancient surgeries, optical technology, and other amazing abilities. But how do we know if these burial stones are real or fake?

For hundreds of years, burial stones have been directly removed from tombs in Ica, Peru. These ancient artifacts were referenced and even taken back to Spain since the times of the Spanish quest for gold in the 1500s.[1] It is only stones displaying dinosaurs and technology which have been labeled as fakes and forgeries by experts who seek to maintain credibility with the educational establishment. But what does the preponderance of evidence reveal?

Starting in 1966 and continuing into the 1970s, a medical doctor named Javier Cabrera collected and preserved over 11,000 stones, primarily from local grave robbers, who claimed to have collected these burial stones within the extremely dry tombs containing the mummified remains of people from their ancient civilization. None of these burial stones were considered controversial until a significant number started to be found depicting ancient technology or dinosaurs. The stones vary in size (from a few inches in diameter to four feet or more in size); surface finish (from lines scratched through a black finish coating to intricately carved reliefs); and style (from crude drawings to artistically accurate and detailed works of art) – similar to how modern tombstones vary in size and quality. Essentially, all the rocks, whether they show amazing technology or not, exhibit the same thick patina (a slowly developing mineral which oozes out of the rock substrate over time), and appear to have been carved using similar techniques from the same time period. Thus, there is no reason for rejecting stones showing dinosaurs as being anything but authentic - other than a philosophical reluctance to accept ancient mankind as concurrent with dinosaurs and capable of advanced technology. So what excuse do evolutionists use for rejecting the authenticity of burial stones which undermine their belief system?

In 1973-1977, a local farmer named Uschuya claimed to have found these stones within local tombs, which are scattered throughout the region. When later faced with prison on a charge of grave-robbing, he changed his story and claimed that he and a few others had carved the stones. This would mean they carved almost 10,000 stones (more than three per day for 10 years!). But think about the choices he was facing when accused of selling these ancient artifacts. He either had to claim he had carved them himself… or be thrown into a horrible Peruvian prison. He supposedly demonstrated how dentist drills and saw blades could be used to carve counterfeit Ica stones and how baked cow dung could imitate ancient patina.[2] Others have shown how these counterfeits display metal contamination within the grooves and were extremely crude, easy to distinguish, and quite inferior to real burial stones.[3] Furthermore, by carving dinosaurs and technology on the stones they would immediately be suspected as fake by archeological "experts" - lowering their value and giving the forgers no incentive to carve such scenes.

Even though there is no stylistic or physical difference between "real" Ica burial stones and those labeled "fake," even though stones showing dinosaurs have been seen by ancient artifact experts and declared original,[4] even though the stones depict things which could not have been known in the 1970s (such as circular rosettes on dinosaur skin and tails being held aloft when walking), it is immediately claimed that any stone showing a dinosaur is a fake. This is because if dinosaurs were seen by mankind, then 60 - 240 million years of evolutionary "history" vanishes. If these burial stones are real, then it is the story of evolution that turns out to be the real fake, not the burial stones. Thus, the stones have to be declared forgeries – not because of the evidence against them, but in spite of the evidence in their favor.

1000 AD
2000 AD
???
PERU

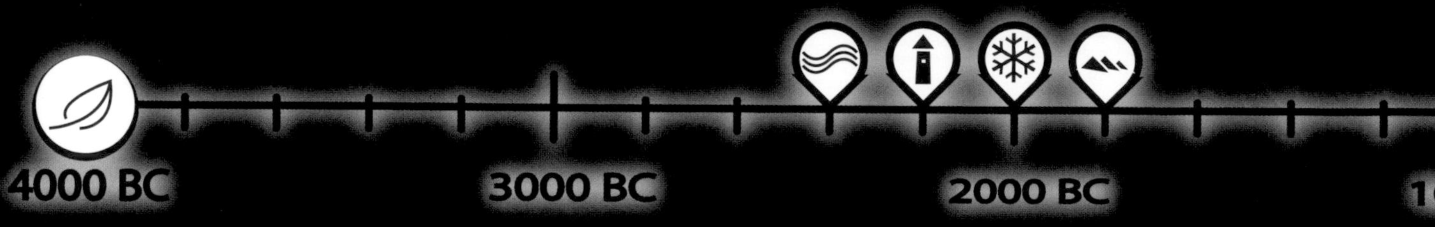

Surgeons of Peru

Burial stones have been removed from tombs around Ica, Peru, which document ancient doctors performing caesarian section births, heart surgery, and a variety of other surgical procedures. Thousands of tombs in this area contain the mummified remains of the deceased along with clothing and other artifacts from their lives. The carved burial stones are believed by many experts to be representative of their lives, and the stones showing medical practices may have been specifically buried with ancient doctors. They may even have been originally used as training tools in ancient "schools of medicine"!

Shown below are several examples of the amazing abilities and technology which were apparently practiced by these ancient people. The stones are assumed to be recent fakes because the ruling paradigm of our age is that ancient people were far too primitive to have practiced the types of medical procedures depicted upon these stones. Yet a forger would be unlikely to take the time and effort required to carve an "out of place" scene such as is shown upon these rocks because it would be immediately suspected as forgery. Producing an artifact depicting a modern scene seems counter-productive. The more logical explanation is the simplest one – these burial stones simply depict real events from the past.

The original brain surgery? Look at the incision point and measurement tool.

Here a surgeon and his "nurse" seem to be doing a stomach/intestinal operation.

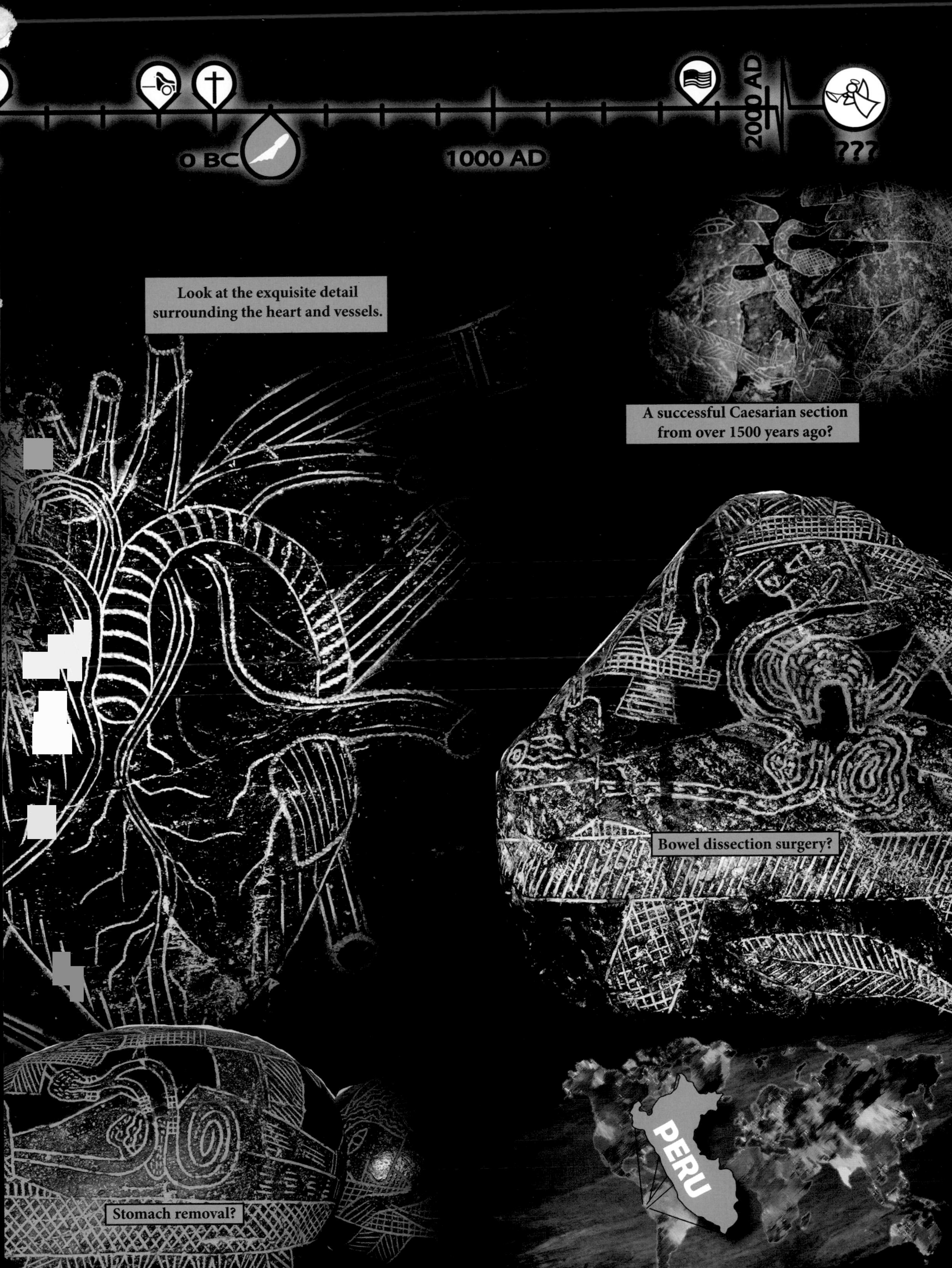

Look at the exquisite detail surrounding the heart and vessels.

A successful Caesarian section from over 1500 years ago?

Bowel dissection surgery?

Stomach removal?

Shake, Rattle, & Roll

China is routinely accused of stealing technology from the West, but China was actually the most technologically advanced nation in the world for more than two thousand years - until the Western world overtook China during the scientific revolution. One example of this is the invention of the instrument used to measure the occurrence, direction, and magnitude of earthquakes – the seismometer. It wasn't until the 18th century that Western scientists started developing a working seismometer, while China invented an operating seismometer 1700 years earlier!

In 132 AD, the "Michelangelo" of ancient China, a famous astronomer, mathematician, inventor, geographer, cartographer, artist, poet, statesman, and literary scholar named Zhang Heng, created an inventive device for not only measuring the occurrence of earthquakes over great distances, but pinpointing the direction in which the earthquake had occurred. This was important for the large geographic areas of ancient Chinese kingdoms because it allowed the emperor to send aid to earthquake-stricken areas. China has been plagued by quakes throughout history. As recently as 1976 an 8.2 Richter scale earthquake in Tangshan killed more than a quarter million people. For that reason, China is a major source of earthquake detection and prediction research. Historical earthquake records are of great interest for understanding both the risk level and patterns over time.

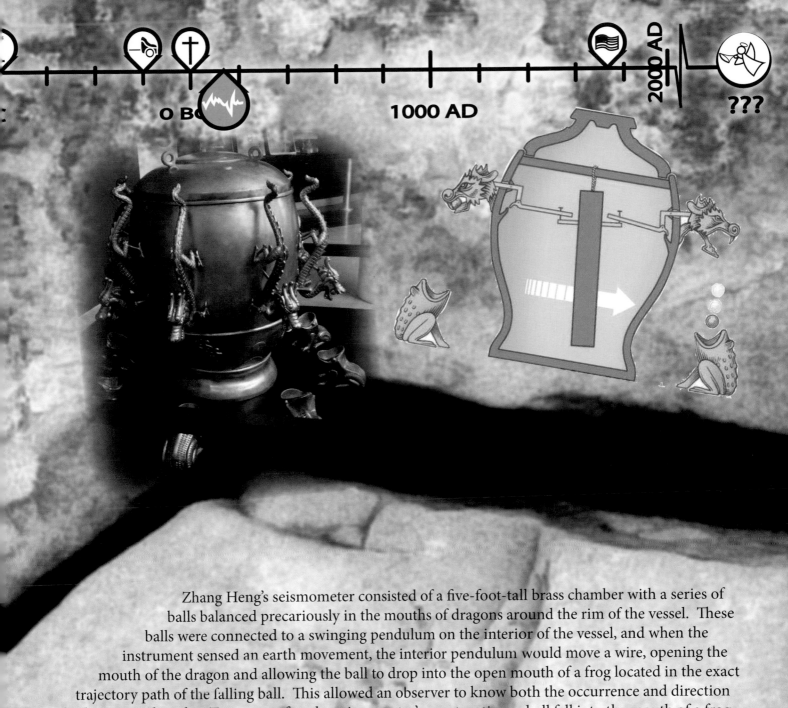

O BC 1000 AD 2000 AD ???

Zhang Heng's seismometer consisted of a five-foot-tall brass chamber with a series of balls balanced precariously in the mouths of dragons around the rim of the vessel. These balls were connected to a swinging pendulum on the interior of the vessel, and when the instrument sensed an earth movement, the interior pendulum would move a wire, opening the mouth of the dragon and allowing the ball to drop into the open mouth of a frog located in the exact trajectory path of the falling ball. This allowed an observer to know both the occurrence and direction of a distant earthquake. Two years after the seismometer's construction, a ball fell into the mouth of a frog even though no one in the capital city had felt an earthquake. Emperor Han's ministers doubted that any quake had occurred. Several days later couriers carrying news of an earthquake arrived from a city hundreds of miles away - in the exact direction Heng's invention had indicated a quake had occurred! As part of their 2006 historic earthquake research work, Feng Rui and Yu Yan-xiang of The Institute of Geophysics (China's earthquake administration) concluded that the earthquake which set off Zhang Heng's seismometer was magnitude 7 in Longxi with an epicenter at Tianshui on December 13, 134 AD.[1]

Not only was the development of this ancient scientific instrument a testimony to the genius and inventiveness of mankind, it is a visual marvel as well – combining beauty, inventiveness, artistry, tradition, and metalwork to create a working scientific tool. All this was accomplished nearly two millennia before modern man finally invented a simliar instrument.

4000 BC 3000 BC 2000 BC 10

Anyone who has ever attempted to make pottery from a lump of clay understands the skill and talent required. To form a perfectly round pot involves spinning (requiring mechanical rotating equipment), wet clay (requiring an understanding of fine clay dispersions), while precisely forming and smoothing the surface with your hands placed inside and outside of the hollow vessel (requiring skill, talent, patience, and perseverance). The thinner the walls of the vessel, the more precise and difficult the process becomes. The manufacturing process is not complete until the clay vessel is decorated (requiring an understanding of paints, pigments, and brushes), and fired (requiring an understanding of high temperature heating and slow cooling processes). The fact that these finely crafted vessels can be found all the way back to the earliest Peruvian and Japanese civilizations 3000 - 4000 years ago, shows that these people had obvious artistic and technical skills immediately after the dispersion from Babel. Furthermore, the extremely thin walls and/or fine craftsmanship of the Peruvian vessels would be difficult for many skilled artisans to achieve even today.

The Japanese pottery shown on this page is dated approximately 3500 years old and shows the skill of even very early potters. Although the Inca pot is estimated to be only 1800 - 2200 years

Dinosaur Pots

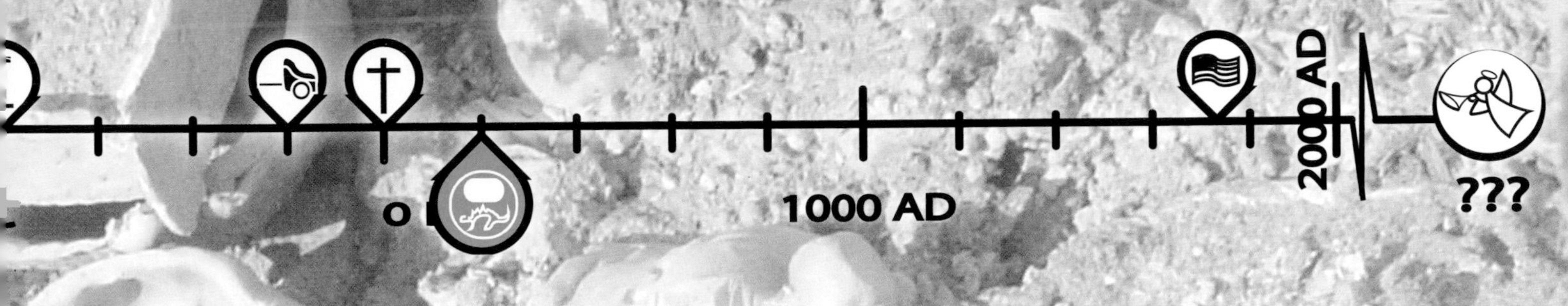

old, it has another interesting feature. Note that the painted design on the Peruvian pot shows a stylistic representation of what are clearly dinosaur-type creatures. If those were the only place these types of representations were found, they could easily be dismissed as imaginative creatures…but when viewed in combination with clear dinosaur representations found on Ica burial stones (see page 14), unfossilized dinosaur tissue (see page 22), and the cultural fixation of the Japanese and Chinese with dragons (i.e. dinosaurs), there is a compelling case that these very skilled humans did, indeed, see or have a cultural remembrance of dinosaurs living with mankind. This fact devastates the belief in the "millions-of-years" time frame needed by evolutionists to hang onto a belief in slowly evolving life over eons of time. The fact that mankind knew of and decorated even their pottery with dinosaurs, testifies that mankind and all animals were created together at the beginning of time – mere thousands, not millions, of years ago.

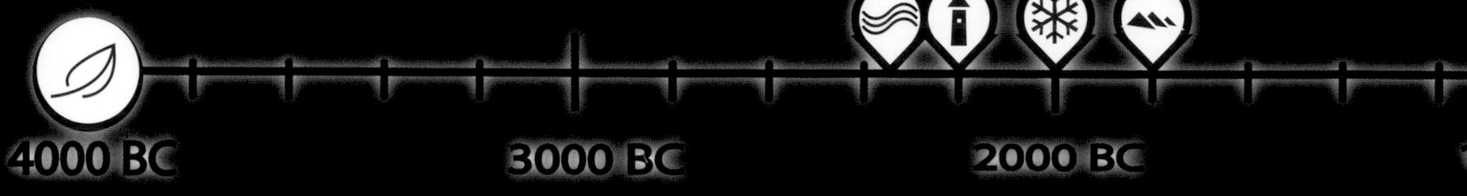

MACHU PICCHU

The indisputable king of modern architects is Frank Lloyd Wright. Yet few structures he designed will remain standing 500 years from now. Contrast this with the monumental achievement of the ancient Incas, who built an entire city complex, located 8000 feet above sea level atop one of the most inaccessible mountains on the planet. Dubbed in the year 2000 as one of the remaining top ten wonders of the ancient world, Machu Picchu is by far the most visited attraction in all of Peru.

This city was apparently built as a royal vacation residence for the Inca emperors and was inhabited for over 100 years before being abandoned in 1572. The city had a permanent population of 300 - 1,000 people. But it is the civil engineering of the city which is most astounding.[1] Among the many wonders of this stone city:

- Water is supplied via an ingeniously designed canal from a single spring located half a mile away. This water-tight, stone-lined canal sends the water to a series of sixteen fountains winding past both ceremonial and residential sites so that citizens can easily fill vessels with water without going to a river located thousands of feet down the mountain.
- During the winter season, Machu Picchu receives as much as sixteen inches of rain per month, making the high, steep terrain treacherous and susceptible to landslides and erosion. To solve this problem the engineers built intricately designed terraces, which held the soil in place while allowing rapid drainage of water through gravel placed at the bottom of each rock-walled terrace to each succeeding lower level terrace. The urban areas contained storm water channels alongside all steps and paths, which would be the envy of any modern city planner. The large gathering plaza was lined with a subsurface of chipped stone, allowing for rapid drainage and run-off so that citizens would not be standing in a lake of water when ceremonial gatherings corresponded to the rainy season.

- The stonework of the city's walls and buildings was intricate, precise, and durable. The stones were cut to such precision that a sheet of paper cannot be placed between any of the blocks, and they have been locked together without any mortar or cement.
- Doors and windows were laid out in a trapezoidal shape - which maximizes their strength. The entire region is prone to frequent earthquakes, and almost all buildings constructed by European occupiers have long since been destroyed by earth movement, whereas this ancient Inca city stands unchanged and unaffected over 550 years after its construction.
- The Inca trail, covering almost 3000 miles of rugged mountainous terrain connecting Machu Picchu to the rest of the Inca Empire, ran along mountain ridges and consisted of stairways and stone pathways.
- The rock walls of the dwellings were covered with a fine plaster, up to one inch thick, made from various colors of clay mixed with water and spread over the surface of the rock. Thus the interior of the rooms would have looked and felt as comfortable as a modern drywall-covered living room.

Although Machu Picchu was not built as early in mankind's history as many of the wonders documented in this book, it drew upon knowledge from previous generations, and much of the engineering ability displayed by its builders exceeded the knowledge used in European cities of the same age.

PERU

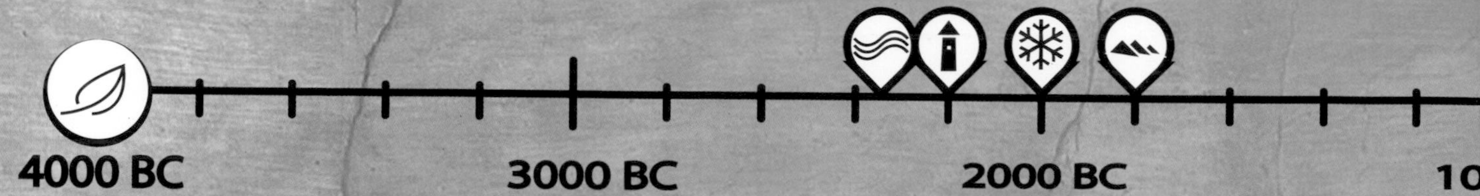

MANKIND: made in the image of GOD

Genesis 1:26-27 states FOUR times that man has been made in the image of God. The Bible claims repeatedly that every word has been inspired by God himself - implying that He has protected its accuracy throughout time (Mark 13:31 - *"Heaven and Earth shall pass away: but my words shall not pass away."* and 2 Timothy 3:16 - *"All Scripture is God-breathed..."*). When God repeats something over and over again, perhaps it is because the knowledge is extremely important and God knows it will be ignored or distorted in the future. He wants the truth that we were *"made in His image"* to be emphatically crystal-clear. I would not be surprised if mankind, *"made in the image of God,"* is repeated four times because there are four major characteristics of mankind which are possessed only by our Creator. Here is my list of four unique characteristics of humanity which do not seem to be shared by any other creature in the universe (except God himself):

- **Mankind is incredibly creative.** No other creature is capable of such phenomenal ingenuity and intelligence. Only mankind can transform materials into the vast array of products, machines, and tools which fill the world. Only mankind is capable of producing beauty and artistry starting purely from his imagination.

- **Mankind is capable of complex communication.** God made mankind to fellowship with Him. No animal can produce complex written and spoken languages. No animal can assign meaning to symbolic scribbling and describe the world around it with passion and meaning.

- **Mankind is capable of love, compassion, and mercy.** Although these characteristics are often ignored or twisted by our fallen nature, we still possess this capacity and, when exercised, these capabilities lift us far above the instinct-driven animal kingdom.

- **Finally, mankind has been given the freedom to choose.** Animals are almost entirely ruled by instincts. They are, in essence, biological robots. Mankind, like God, can choose what he wants to do. This is also the essence of love. Without freedom to choose, there can be no love.

Sadly, all of these characteristics have become distorted by our rebellion against God. A fallen humanity uses its creativity to wage war, build weapons, and steal from others. We use communication to produce pornography and curse our Maker and Savior.

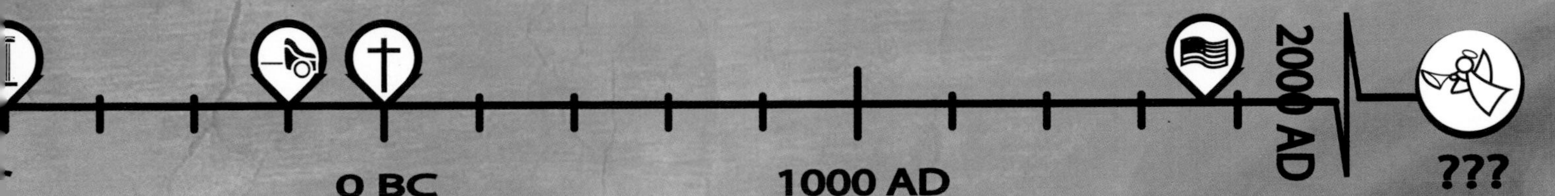

We turn love into hate, compassion into apathy, and mercy into cruelty. We use our free will to ignore the very existence of God - training generation after generation of young minds to ignore God and make their own rules and reality, eventually reaching the point that many cannot comprehend the reality of His existence even when faced with overwhelming evidence from history and creation that the Bible is absolutely true and accurate. When faced with such entrenched one-sided propaganda and indoctrination, which blinds people around us to a truly Biblical viewpoint, what can we do?

Share the truth.

People still have the freedom to choose the truth, - but they first must hear the truth. Jesus still has the ability to heal the intellectually blind, but they must first be exposed to the truth. Millions of people will never hear the Biblical view of history because no one has ever taken the time to explain it to them in a credible way. Hopefully, *Brilliant* can be used in a small way to place mankind's true history in front of people blinded to this reality.

Will we be ridiculed as we share the Bible's account of history? Yes. Will we be persecuted and excluded from mainstream educational and informational outlets when we question the millions-of-years paradigm ruling our age? Yes. But God has a way of using our sacrifice, honoring our obedience, and changing lives in the process.

END | a word about the OF TIME

As readers have pondered the amazing abilities of mankind showcased on each page of this book, they also may have noticed that the timeline on each page ends not in a forward pointing arrowhead (like most timelines), but in a specific event symbolizing the return of Christ. There are far more predictions and promises in both the Old and New Testaments of the Bible concerning the second coming (or return) of Jesus Christ than there are about God's initial visit into creation almost 2000 years ago.[1] Because the Bible describes this event as proceded by a seven-year period of extreme economic, environmental, and cosmic upheaval, this coming period of earth history is largely feared, denied, and/or ignored.

It is beyond the scope of this work to dogmatically predict the timing of future events. Furthermore, the controversy over the millenial reign of Christ and the timing of events during the tribulation period is not the focus of this book, nor does arguing over these issues draw non-believers toward the love and salvation which Christ has to offer - especially when we display a lack of brotherly tolerance over differences concerning these Biblical "end-time" issues. However, if even the mention of coming events like *tribulation, end-times, the return of Christ*, or *the rapture* (Matthew 24:3-44) causes apprehension - rather than anticipating the future with excitement and trust - perhaps you need to understand the Bibical timeline of this book more clearly.

Because there was a beginning of time (not so long ago), there will be a wrapping up of history (not so far into the future). Because there is a Creator who personally entered into

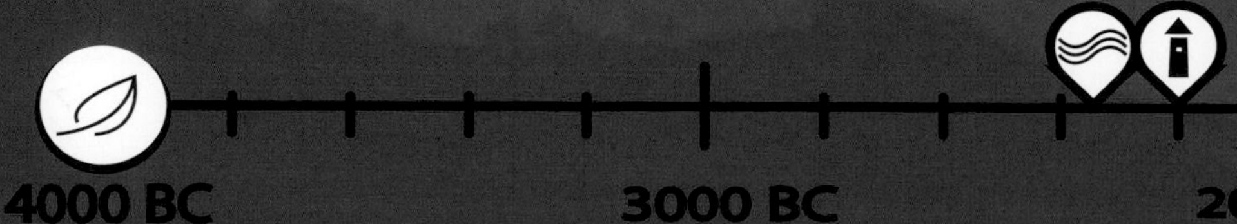

creation, we can come to know and trust the One who made everything (including us). Because humanity is responsible for what is wrong with creation, we cannot blame God for the death, disease, and problems we see all around us. And because this God entered into creation, He understands our struggles and worries, our temptations and failures, our pain and guilt. He took the cost of our rebellion upon himself (death), and provided assurance of victory and reconciliation with our Creator by rising from the dead. We, too, can have victory over both sin and the result of sin (which is death).

There is nothing to fear about the end of time for anyone who has accepted the sacrifice of Jesus on his behalf, because as soon as we accept what He did in our place - giving His very life for us - we are forgiven and reconciled to the One who created us. That does not make us perfect, but it does make us forgiven. Furthermore, because time is part of the physical universe, the Creator who made this universe is outside of time (as we measure and understand it). He knew us before the universe was even created (Jeremaih 1:5). Our Creator and Redeemer is perfectly capable of restoring our physical bodies and everything in the universe back to its original perfection at the conclusion of time.

By truly understanding and believing the Biblical timeline, all fear and trepidation over end times fades like a mist. It is my hope that the information contained within *Brilliant* has moved your understanding of truth and reality in that direction.

This timeline is a reality.

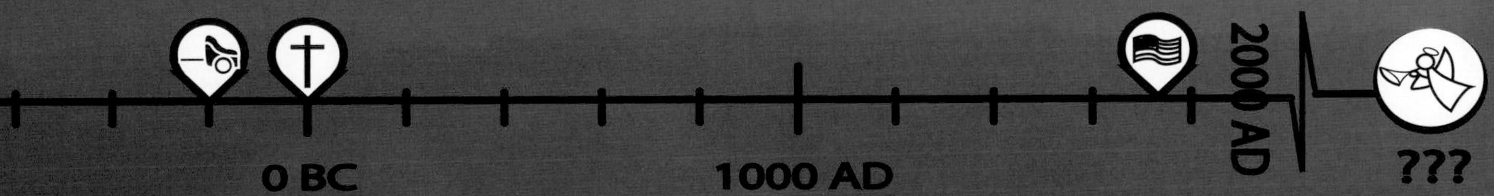

Page 7: Bruce Malone, *Censored Science*, Search for the Truth Publications, 2009, 97.

Page 12: Stephen Brennecke, The Bronze Tree of Sanxingdui: the Oldest man-made Genesis Artifact?, *Journal of Creation*, 20(2), 2006.

Page 16: C.H Kang & Ethel Nelson, *The Discovery of Genesis: How the Truths of Genesis Were Found Hidden in the Chinese Language*, Concordia House Publishing, 1979.

Page 18: 1. William Corliss, *Archeological Anomalies: Small Artifacts,* The Sourcebook Project, 2003, 249.
2. William Corliss, p. 430-432,438-446.

Page 20: 1. *Report on British Fossil Reptiles Parts I & II, Report of the British Association for the Advancement of Science,* Plymouth, England, 1842.
2. Rick Deighton, *More than Conquerors in Cultural Clashes*, Search for the Truth Publications, 2014, 49-50.

Page 22: *Science Direct*, Volume 115, Issue 6, July 2013, 603–608.

Page 24: David May, http://mineralwellsindex.com, 2008.

Page 28: 1. David Menton, *A Pocket Guide to Apemen: Separating Fact from Fiction*, Answers in Genesis, 2010, 20.
2. Evan Hadingham, *Neanderthals Defy Stereotypes,* NOVA, http://www.pbs.org/wgbh/nova/evolution/defy-stereotypes.html, posted 1/9/13.

Page 30: http://en.wikipedia.org/wiki/Lascaux , posted 12/1/13.

Page 32: 1. "History in the Remaking," *Newsweek*, 2/18/10.
2. Andrew Collins, *Gobekli Tepe:Genesis of the Gods: The Temple of the Watchers and the Discovery of Eden*, 2014, Bear & Co.

Page 34: 1. http://whc.unesco.org/en/list/138, posted 9/1/14.
2. http://www.adventurecorps.com/archaeo/collapse.html, posted 9/1/14.
3. http://san.beck.org/EC-index.html, posted 9/1/14

Page 36: 1. John Ashton, *Unwrapping the Pharaohs: How Egyptian Archaeology Confirms the Biblical Timeline,* Master Books, 2006.
2. http://hermeneutics.stackexchange.com/questions/4686/why-did-the-masoretes-take-away-100-or-50-years-from-the-age-of-the-fathers-at, posted 7/1/14.
3. Bruce Malone, *Censored Science*, third ed. , Search for the Truth Publications, 2013, 96-97.
4. Anne Habermehl, *Proceedings of the 7th International Conference on Creationism*, Ancient Egypt, The Ice Age, and Biblical Chronology, Aug. 2013.
5. Anne Habermehl, *Proceedings of the 7th International Conference on Creationism*, Revising Egyptian Chronology: Joseph as Imhotep and Amenemhat IV as Pharaoh of the Exodus, Aug. 2013.

Page 38: 1. http://en.wikipedia.org/wiki/List_of_people_with_the_most_children, posted 9/1/14.
2. http://www.reshafim.org.il/ad/egypt/people/index.html, posted 9/1/14.

Page 40: 1. http://www.genesisveracityfoundation.com/submerged.html, posted 7/1/14.
2. James Nienhuis, *Ice Age Civilizations,* The Book Connection Publications, 2006, 1-12.

Page 44: 1. http://en.wikipedia.org/wiki/Piri_Reis_map, posted 9/1/14.
2. http://www.ancientdestructions.com/piri-reis-map-of-antarctica/, posted 9/1/14.

Page 46: 1. John Ashton, *Unwrapping the Pharaohs: How Egyptian Archaeology Confirms the Biblical Timeline,* Master Books, 2006.
2. http://www.math.nus.edu.sg/aslaksen/gem-projects/hm/0102-1-pyramids/page1002.htm, 4/31/14.

Page 48: 1. Philip Coppens, *The Lost Civilization Enigma*, New Page Books, 2013, 38-60.
2. Coppens, 31-38.
3. Meg Greene, *The Technology of Ancient Japan*, Rosen Publishing Group, 2006.
4. Fabio Bourdon, et.al., *Lost Civilizations: Rediscovering the Great Cultures of the Past,* Barnes & Noble, 1998, 282-340.

Page 50: http://www.history.com/topics/maya, posted 8/1/14.

Page 52: 1. http://en.wikipedia.org/wiki/Iron_Age, posted 6/1/14.
2. Sir William Flinders Petrie, *The Pyramids and Temples of Gihez,* Scribner & William, 1883, 171.
3. Christopher Dunn, *The Giza Power Plant: Technologies of Egypyt*, Bear & Co, 1998, 49-66.
4. Donald Chittick, *The Puzzle of Ancient Man: Evidence for Advanced Tech. in Past Civilizations,* Creation Compass, 2006, 108-126.
5. Dunn, 67-92.

Page 54: 1. Meg Greene, The Technology of Ancient Japan, , Rosen Central, 2006, 5-10.
2. Greene, 35, 18-19.
3. Greene, 22-24.

Page 56: 1. Donald Chittick, *The Puzzle of Ancient Man: Evidence for Advanced Tech. in Past Civilizations,* Creation Compass, 2006, 81-94.
2. Robert Temple, *The Crystal Sun: Rediscovering the Lost Technology of the Ancient World*, Arrow Books, 2000, 246.
3. http://arts.cultural-china.com/en/70Arts10318.html, posted 8/10/14.

Page 58: Saydi Maria Negron Romero, *Presenting Peru and Machupicchu*, Traea Asociacion Grafica Educativa, 2012.

Page 62: 1. Philip Coppens, *The Lost Civilization Enigma*, New Page Books, 2013, 109-115.
2. en.m.wikipedia.org/wiki/copper/,posted 7/1/14.
3. William Corliss, *Ancient Man: A Handbook of Puzzling Artifacts,* The Sourcebook Project, 1978, 341-345.
4. Henry Hodges, *Technology in the Ancient World*, Borzoi Books, 1970, p.195-207.

Page 64: Saydi M. Negron Romero, *Presenting Peru & Machu Picchu,* Tarea Asociacion Grafica Educativa, 2012, 48.

Page 66: 1. http://great-wall-marathon.com/great-wall-of-china, posted 5/1/14

2. Robert Greenerger, *The Technology of Ancient China,* Rosen Publishing Group, 2006.
3. http://abcnews.go.com/blogs/headlines/2012/07/great-wall-of-china-longer-than-previously-reported/, posted 6/1/14.
4. http://en.wikipedia.org/wiki/Rudder, posted 8/1/14.

Page 68: Charles Mann, *1491:New Revelations of the Americas Before Columbus*, Borzoi Books, 2005, 3-12.

Page 70: 1. Frank Joseph, *The Lost Worlds of Ancient America,* New Page Books, 2012, 215-221.
2. http://en.wikipedia.org/wiki/Stone_spheres_of_Costa_Rica, posted 5/1/14.
3. Frank Joseph, *The Lost Worlds of Ancient America,* New Page Books, 2012, 215-220.

Page 72: 1. Agnes Hooper Gottlieb, et.al., *1,000 Years, 1,000 People: Ranking the Men and Women Who Shaped the Millennium*, 1998.
2. Lionel Casson, et,al., *Mysteries of the Past,* American Heritage publishing, 1977, 90-91.
3. http://en.wikipedia.org/wiki/Phaistos_disk, posted 1/23/14.
4. Jerome Eisenberg, *Minerva Magazine,* The Phaistos Disk: A One-Hundred-Year-Old Hoax?, July/Aug. 2008, 9-24.

Page 74: 1. Barry Fell, *America B.C.*, Artisan Publishers, 1989.
2. Fell,113-124.

Page 76: 1. http://en.wikipedia.org/wiki/Serpent_Mound, posted 5/1/14.
2. Stephen Shaffer, Voices of the Ancients, Council Press, 2012, 69-74.
3. R.B. Etzenhouser, *Engravings of prehistoric specimens from Michigan*, 1910.
4. Lisa Young, *Museums: Michigan's Mystery Relics*, http://archive.archaeology.org/0405/reviews/michigan.html, posted 6/4/14.
5. Etzenhouser, 32.

Page 80: 1. Robert Johnson, *The Parthenon Code: Mankind's History in Marble*, Solving Light Books, 2005, 1-30.
2. Johnson, 24.

Page 82: Robert Johnson, *The Parthenon Code: Mankind's History in Marble*, Solving Light Books, 2005, 12-16.

Page 84: 1. Tom Chao, *Mystery of Greek Amphitheater's Amazing Sound Finally Solved*, 2007, http://www.livescience.com/7269-mystery-greek-amphitheater-amazing-sound-finally-solved.html, posted Jan. 2014.
2. *Journal of the Acoustics Society of America*, 2007.

Page 86: 1. http://en.wikipedia.org/wiki/List_of_countries_by_life_expectancy, posted 7/1/14.
2. Brian Cotterell, *Mechanics of pre-industrial technology*, Cambridge University Press., ISBN 978-0-521-42871-2, 2011, 127.

Page 87: 3. Nanthia Suthana, et.al, Memory Enhancement and Deep-Brain Stimulation of the Entorhinal Area, *N Engl J Med*, 2012.

Page 89: 1. http://theawesomecoolstuff.wordpress.com/2013/05/01/25-most-intense-archaeological-discoveries-in-human-history/, posted Nov. 2013.
2. http://www.world-mysteries.com/sar_11.htm, posted Nov. 2013.
3. Robert John Van Risseghem, *Tables of the Moneychangers*, 2008.
4. http://en.wikipedia.org/wiki/MythBusters_(2005_season)#Baghdad_Battery, posted Nov. 2013.

Page 92: 1. Saydi Maria Negron Romero, *Presenting Peru & Machu Picchu*, Traea Asociacion Grafica Educativa, 2012.
2. Dennis Swift, *Secrets of the Ica Stones and Nazca Lines*, 2006.
3. http://whc.unesco.org/en/list/700,posted 9/1/14.

Page 94: 1. Roberto Ciarla , *The Eternal Army: The Terracotta Soldiers of the First Emperor,* White Star Publications, 2012.
2. http://en.wikipedia.org/wiki/Terracotta_Army , posted 12/1/13.
3. Brook Larmer, *National Geographic Magazine*, Terra-Cotta Warriors in Color, June 2012 , 74-87.

Page 96: 1. http://www.ipst.gatech.edu/amp/collection/museum_invention_paper.htm, posted 2/26/14.
2. Robert Greenberger, *The Technology of Ancient China*, The Rosen Publishing Group, 2006, 15-18.

Page 98: 1. http://en.wikipedia.org/wiki/Library_of_Alexandria, posted 4/1/2014.

Page 100: 1. http://en.wikipedia.org/wiki/Ajanta_Caves, posted 12/1/13.
2. Benoy K. Behl, *The Ajanta Caves: Ancient Paintings of Buddhist India,* Thames & Hudson, 2005.

Page 102: 1. http://en.wikipedia.org/wiki/Antikythera_mechanism#cite_note-SEAMANR.C3.B6ssler2011-2 , Posted 12/1/13.
2. Johnston, Ian, Device that let Greeks decode solar system, *The Scotsman*, 2006.
3. Eric G. Swedin; David L. Ferro, *Computers: The Life Story of a Technology,* ISBN 978-0-8018-8774-1, posted 5/28/13.

Page 104: 1. Gian Quasar, *Baalbek: A Colossal Enigma*, http://www.bibliotecapleyades.net/esp_baalbek_1.htm, posted 7/1/14.
2. Mike Heisler, *Aliens Debunked: Baalbek,* , http://ancientaliensdebunked.com/references-and-transcripts/baalbek/, posted 7/1/14.

Page 110: 1. Dennis Swift, *Secrets of the Ica Stones and Nazca Lines*, 2006.
2. http://en.wikipedia.org/wiki/Ica_stones, posted 2/1/14.
3. Swift, *Secrets of the Ica Stones and Nazca Lines*, 2006.
4. Swift , *"The Mystery of the Ica Stones: Did Man Walk with Dinosaurs?,"* retrieved Sept. 12, 2011 from http://www.dinosaursandman.com//research/Fortean_Times_Rebuttal.pdf, 4-13

Page 114: 1. www.ilookchina.net/2011/07/24/ancient-chinese-inventions-that-changed-the-world/.
2. Robert Greenberger, *The Technology of Ancient China*, 2006, Rosen Publishing, 24-25.

Page 118: Kenneth Wright and Alfredo Zegarra, *Machu Picchu: A Civil Engineering Marvel*, ASCE Press, 2000.

Page 122: Chuck Missler, *Hidden Treasures of the Biblical Text*, Koinonia House, 2000.

About the Author

Bruce Malone has 27 years of research experience with the Dow Chemical Company. He has a BA in Chemical Engineering from the University of Cincinnati and holds 17 patents for new products with Dow. In 2008, Bruce retired to work as full time director of Search for the Truth Ministries with the vision of *"Awakening Hearts and Minds to Biblical Truth"*. Search for the Truth has printed and distributed over 200,000 books - primarily to students and prisoners. *Brilliant* is his sixth book dealing with the evidence for creation.

Bruce travels widely and has given over 600 presentations on the scientific evidence supporting the reality of our recent creation throughout schools, churches, and universities in 12 countries. He has served as an adjunct speaker for the Institute for Creation Research and is an associate speaker for Logos Research Associates. Bruce and his wife Robin have been married for 32 years, have 4 children (Michael, Marc, Margaret, and Matthew) and three grandchildren (Corrie, Eleanor, and Lillian). They reside in Midland, MI.

SHARE THE TRUTH AND SAVE!

Science & the Bible

Is your science being Censored? Learn about how science actually confirms the Bible's account of creation.
128 pgs
Full Color
Hardcover

Evidence for Creation

Scientific evidence for creation for every single day of the year. A daily devotional.
408 pgs

History & the Bible

Learn how history from all over the world points to and supports a biblical timeline.
128 pgs
Full Color
Hardcover

Daily Devotional

Illustrated sequel with MORE evidence for creation. An article for 365 days! Beautifully designed.
408 pgs

Any 1 book = $12 **2-9 books = $9/ea.**

10+ books, $6 each!

(mix & match, priced to give away)

Resource	Qty.	Cost each (see above)	Total
		Subtotal	
		Shipping	
		MI Residents: add 6% sales tax	
		TOTAL ENCLOSED	

SHIPPING:
1 bk. add $3, 2-9 bks. add $2/ea., 10+ bks. add $1.50/ea.

Return order form to:

Search for the Truth
3275 Monroe Rd.
Midland, MI 48642

or CALL
989-837-5546

SHIP ORDER TO:

Name: ____________________ Phone: ____________

Street: ____________________

Town, ST, Zip: ____________________